The Manifestation Code

AF369031

The Manifestation Code

Attracting Wealth, Health, and Happiness

Aria Rivers

Mindful Pages

Published in 2024

ISBN: 9789358812350 (PB)
ISBN: 9789358812527 (eBook)

Published by

Mindful Pages
Imprint of Alpha Editions LLC
312 W. 2nd St #1834
Casper, WY 82601, USA
www.mindfulpagespublishers.com

All rights reserved. No part of this publication may be reproduced, distributed, or transmitted in any form or by any means, including photocopying, recording, or other electronic or mechanical methods, without the prior written permission of the publisher, except in the case of brief quotations embodied in critical reviews and specific other non-commercial uses permitted by copyright law.

Table of Contents

Introduction

In a world where the pursuit of happiness and fulfillment seems endless, the concept of manifestation offers a beacon of hope and possibility. At its core, manifestation is the practice of harnessing the power of intention to create the reality we desire. It's about aligning our thoughts, beliefs, and actions with our deepest desires and goals to attract abundance in all aspects of life. From financial prosperity to vibrant health and harmonious relationships, manifestation holds the key to unlocking our fullest potential and transforming our lives in profound ways.

But what exactly is manifestation, and how does it work? At its essence, manifestation is grounded in the universal principle known as the Law of Attraction. This law posits that like attracts like, meaning that the energy we emit into the universe through our thoughts, feelings, and actions is mirrored back to us in the form of our reality. In other words, what we focus on expands, and by consciously directing our attention and intention towards our goals, we can actively shape our reality and manifest our desires into existence.

Central to the practice of manifestation is the power of intention. Intention is the driving force behind all creation, the catalyst that propels our desires from the realm of possibility into tangible reality. When we set clear and focused intentions, we signal to the universe what we want to manifest in our lives, thereby activating the Law of Attraction and drawing our desires towards us with greater ease and efficiency.

But intention alone is not enough. To truly harness the power of manifestation, we must align our thoughts, beliefs, and actions with our intentions. This means cultivating a positive mindset, free from limiting beliefs and self-doubt, and cultivating a sense of unwavering faith and belief in the inherent abundance of the universe. It means taking inspired action towards our goals, trusting in the process, and remaining open to unexpected opportunities and synchronicities that may arise along the way.

The transformative potential of manifestation is profound and far-reaching. By consciously directing our thoughts and intentions towards our goals, we can literally rewire our brains and reprogram our subconscious minds for success and abundance. Studies have shown that practices such as visualization, affirmation, and gratitude can have a profound impact on our mental and emotional well-being, leading to increased feelings of happiness, fulfillment, and overall life satisfaction.

But the benefits of manifestation extend beyond our mental and emotional realms. When we align ourselves with the energy of abundance, we open ourselves up to a world of infinite possibilities and opportunities. We become magnetic to the people, resources, and circumstances that can help us achieve our goals, and we experience a sense of flow and synchronicity that guides us effortlessly towards our desires.

In essence, manifestation is not just about getting what we want; it's about becoming who we were meant to be. It's about stepping into our power as conscious creators of our reality and embracing our innate ability to shape our destinies according to our deepest desires and aspirations. It's about realizing that we are co-creators of our lives, and that the power to manifest our dreams lies within each and every one of us.

Manifestation is not merely a passive process of wishful thinking; it requires active participation and engagement with our deepest desires and aspirations. It invites us to step into our power as conscious creators and take ownership of our lives. By aligning our thoughts, beliefs, and actions with our intentions, we can begin to manifest the life of our dreams with clarity and purpose.

One of the key principles of manifestation is the concept of vibration. Everything in the universe, including our thoughts and emotions, emits a certain frequency or vibration. When we focus on positive thoughts and emotions, we raise our vibration and become more aligned with the energy of abundance. Conversely, when we dwell on negativity and lack, we lower our vibration and attract more of the same into our lives.

Understanding the role of vibration in manifestation empowers us to take control of our energy and consciously shift our focus towards thoughts and feelings that support our desires. By cultivating a sense of joy, gratitude, and abundance in our lives, we can elevate our vibration and magnetize our intentions with greater potency and efficiency.

Moreover, manifestation is not limited to material wealth or external achievements; it encompasses all aspects of our being, including our physical health, emotional well-being, and spiritual fulfillment. When we set intentions for holistic abundance, we create a ripple effect that permeates every area of our lives, leading to greater balance, harmony, and overall fulfillment.

In the journey of manifestation, patience and trust are paramount. It's essential to recognize that manifestation operates according to divine timing, and that our desires may not always manifest in the way or timeframe we expect. By surrendering to the flow of life and trusting in the wisdom of the universe, we allow for miracles to unfold in ways we never imagined possible.

Ultimately, manifestation is a co-creative process between ourselves and the universe. By aligning our intentions with the energy of abundance and taking inspired action towards our goals, we can manifest a reality that reflects our deepest desires and aspirations. In the process, we discover the profound truth that we are powerful creators capable of shaping our destinies according to our highest vision.

Manifestation is a transformative practice that holds the power to unlock our fullest potential and create a life of abundance, joy, and fulfillment. By harnessing the power of intention, aligning with the energy of abundance, and trusting in the process, we can manifest our dreams into reality and experience the profound magic of co-creating with the universe. So, dare to dream big, believe in yourself, and embark on the journey of manifestation with an open heart and mind. Your greatest desires are waiting to be manifested – all you have to do is believe.

In the pages of this book the readers will embark on a journey of self-discovery and empowerment. They will learn practical techniques and exercises for harnessing the power of manifestation to attract abundance in all areas of their lives, from financial prosperity to radiant health and fulfilling relationships. They will discover the profound impact their thoughts and beliefs have on their reality, and they will gain the tools and insights they need to consciously create the life of their dreams.

Chapter 1: Understanding the Law of Attraction

The Law of Attraction has captivated the minds of millions worldwide, offering a glimpse into the profound connection between our thoughts and the reality we experience. In this article, we will embark on a journey to explore the intricacies of the Law of Attraction, from its definition and basic principles to its historical roots and core concepts. By unraveling the mysteries of this universal law, we can unlock the power to manifest our deepest desires and transform our lives.

At its core, the Law of Attraction is a universal principle that states: like attracts like. In other words, the thoughts, emotions, and beliefs we hold emit a certain vibration that draws similar energy back to us. Put simply, positive thoughts attract positive outcomes, while negative thoughts attract negative outcomes.

The Law of Attraction operates on the premise that we are all connected to an infinite field of energy, often referred to as the universe or the quantum field. Through our thoughts and emotions, we interact with this energy field and shape our reality accordingly. By consciously directing our thoughts and focusing on what we want rather than what we don't want, we can harness the power of the Law of Attraction to manifest our desires.

While the Law of Attraction has gained widespread popularity in recent years, its roots can be traced back to ancient spiritual and philosophical teachings. Ancient civilizations such as the Egyptians, Greeks, and Hindus all recognized the power of the mind to influence reality and achieve desired outcomes.

In more modern times, the concept of the Law of Attraction experienced a resurgence with the New Thought movement in the late 19th and early 20th centuries. Figures such as Phineas Quimby, Mary Baker Eddy, and Napoleon Hill explored the principles of mind over matter and the power of positive thinking.

The Law of Attraction gained further prominence with the release of the book "The Secret" by Rhonda Byrne in 2006. This best-selling book introduced millions of readers to the idea that thoughts have the power to create reality, sparking a global phenomenon and igniting interest in manifestation practices.

Core Concepts

Several key concepts underpin the Law of Attraction and contribute to its efficacy in manifesting desires:

> Intention: Setting clear intentions is the first step in harnessing the power of the Law of Attraction. By defining what we want to manifest and why it's important to us, we send a clear signal to the universe and align ourselves with our desired outcomes.

> Vibration: Everything in the universe, including our thoughts and emotions, emits a certain vibration. By cultivating positive thoughts and emotions, we raise our vibrational frequency and become magnetic to positive experiences and opportunities.

> Manifestation: Manifestation is the process of bringing our desires into reality through the power of our thoughts and intentions. By visualizing our goals, feeling the emotions associated with achieving them, and taking inspired action, we can manifest our dreams into tangible results.

Understanding these core concepts is essential for effectively applying the Law of Attraction in our lives. By aligning our thoughts, emotions, and beliefs with our desires, we can tap into the infinite potential of the universe and create the life we envision.

The Law of Attraction offers a profound insight into the power of the mind to shape our reality and manifest our desires. By understanding its definition, historical background, and core concepts, we can unlock the secrets to harnessing its transformative potential.

As we embark on this journey of exploration and self-discovery, let us remember that the Law of Attraction is not just a theory or belief system – it is a universal law that governs the very fabric of our existence. By embracing its principles and applying them in our daily lives, we can unlock the limitless possibilities that lie within us and create a life filled with abundance, joy, and fulfillment. So, dare to dream big, believe in yourself, and trust in the power of the Law of Attraction to manifest your wildest dreams.

Exploring the Neuroscience and Quantum Physics of Manifestation

Manifestation has long been regarded as a mystical or spiritual practice, but recent advancements in science have shed new light on its mechanisms and efficacy. In this article, we will delve into the science behind manifestation, exploring the fascinating insights provided by neuroscience, psychology, and quantum physics. By understanding the scientific principles at play, we can gain deeper insights into the manifestation process and unlock its transformative potential.

Scientific research in fields such as neuroscience and psychology provides compelling evidence for the principles of manifestation. Neuroscientists have discovered that the brain is highly adaptable and capable of rewiring itself in response to experience, a phenomenon known as neuroplasticity.

Psychological studies have demonstrated the profound impact of thoughts and beliefs on emotions, behaviors, and ultimately, outcomes. By examining the neural mechanisms underlying cognition and emotion, researchers have uncovered the intricate interplay between the mind and the brain, validating the idea that thoughts can shape reality.

Neuroplasticity is the brain's remarkable ability to reorganize and adapt in response to experience. This phenomenon challenges the traditional view of the brain as a fixed and unchangeable organ, demonstrating that it is highly adaptable and responsive to environmental stimuli.

Research has shown that repetitive thoughts and behaviors can lead to changes in brain structure and function, ultimately shaping our perceptions, beliefs, and behaviors. By consciously directing our thoughts and focusing on positive outcomes, we can harness the power of neuroplasticity to rewire our brains for manifestation.

Neurotransmitters and hormones play a crucial role in mediating the effects of thoughts and emotions on the brain and body. Dopamine, often referred to as the "feel-good" neurotransmitter, is involved in reward processing and motivation.

When we experience positive thoughts and emotions, such as joy and excitement, dopamine levels in the brain increase, reinforcing the neural pathways associated with these experiences. This, in turn, enhances our motivation and drive to pursue our goals, making manifestation more effortless and enjoyable.

Similarly, hormones such as oxytocin and serotonin also play a role in manifestation by modulating mood and social bonding. Oxytocin, often called the "love hormone," promotes feelings of trust and connection, while serotonin regulates mood and emotional well-being.

Quantum physics introduces a paradigm-shifting perspective on manifestation, suggesting that consciousness plays a fundamental role in shaping reality. According to quantum theory, the observer effect posits that the act of observing a phenomenon can influence its outcome, highlighting the interconnectedness of mind and matter.

Principles such as entanglement and non-locality further challenge our traditional understanding of reality, suggesting that particles can be connected across vast distances instantaneously. This implies that our thoughts and intentions have the potential to influence events far beyond our immediate surroundings, opening up a realm of infinite possibilities for manifestation.

The science behind manifestation offers a fascinating glimpse into the interconnectedness of mind, brain, and reality. By understanding the principles of neuroscience, psychology, and quantum physics, we can gain deeper insights into the manifestation process and unlock its transformative potential.

As we continue to explore the science of manifestation, let us remember that we are not passive observers of reality, but active participants in its creation. By harnessing the power of our thoughts, emotions, and beliefs, we can shape our destiny and manifest the life of our dreams. So, dare to dream big, believe in yourself, and embrace the limitless possibilities that lie within you.

Real-Life Applications of the Law of Attraction

The Law of Attraction is not merely a theoretical concept but a powerful tool that individuals around the world have successfully wielded to manifest their deepest desires. In this article, we will explore practical applications of the Law of Attraction, showcasing real-life examples, stories, and case studies that illustrate how individuals have harnessed this universal principle to transform their lives. From relationships to career, health, and finances, we will delve into various areas where the Law of Attraction has been applied with remarkable success, offering practical tips for implementing manifestation techniques in everyday life.

Relationships: Attracting Love and Harmony

One of the most common applications of the Law of Attraction is in the realm of relationships. Many individuals have used manifestation techniques to attract loving, fulfilling partnerships into their lives. For example, Sarah, a single woman tired of unsuccessful relationships, decided to apply the Law of Attraction to find her soulmate. She visualized her ideal partner, focusing on the qualities she desired in a relationship such as love, trust, and mutual respect. Through consistent visualization, affirmations, and taking inspired action, Sarah eventually met her perfect match, proving that love truly does attract love.

Practical Tip: Create a vision board or journal dedicated to your ideal relationship, and spend time each day visualizing yourself in a loving partnership.

Career: Manifesting Success and Abundance

Another area where the Law of Attraction can be applied with remarkable results is in the realm of career and professional success. Consider the story of John, a struggling entrepreneur who was determined to turn his business around. Using manifestation techniques such as affirmations, gratitude practices, and setting clear intentions, John transformed his mindset from one of scarcity to one of abundance. He focused on the opportunities and abundance available to him, rather than dwelling on setbacks or failures. As a result, John's business began to thrive, attracting new clients, partnerships, and opportunities for growth.

Practical Tip: Start each day with a positive affirmation related to your career goals, such as "I am successful and prosperous in my endeavors."

Health and Well-being: Cultivating Wellness from Within

The Law of Attraction can also be a powerful tool for improving health and well-being. Take the example of Lisa, who struggled with chronic health issues for years. Fed up with conventional treatments that offered little relief, Lisa turned to manifestation techniques to heal her body from within. She practiced visualization, affirmations, and gratitude for her body's innate healing abilities. Over time, Lisa experienced a remarkable improvement in her health, demonstrating the profound impact of mindset on physical well-being.

Practical Tip: Practice daily gratitude for your body and its ability to heal and thrive, focusing on areas of wellness rather than illness.

Finances: Attracting Wealth and Prosperity

Finally, the Law of Attraction can be a potent tool for attracting wealth and financial abundance. Consider the case of Mark, who was struggling to make ends meet and was buried in debt. Determined to change his financial situation, Mark immersed himself in the principles of the Law of Attraction. He visualized himself as financially prosperous, feeling the emotions of abundance and gratitude. Through consistent manifestation practices and taking inspired action, Mark attracted new opportunities for income generation, paid off his debts, and achieved financial freedom.

Practical Tip: Create a financial abundance plan, setting clear intentions and goals for attracting wealth and prosperity into your life.

The stories and examples shared above are just a few of the countless instances where individuals have successfully applied the principles of the Law of Attraction to manifest their desires. Whether it's finding love, achieving career success, improving health, or attracting financial abundance, the Law of Attraction offers a powerful framework for creating the life of your dreams.

As you embark on your own manifestation journey, remember that consistency, belief, and aligned action are key. By adopting a positive mindset, setting clear intentions, and taking inspired action towards your goals, you too can harness the transformative power of the Law of Attraction to manifest miracles in your own life. So, dare to dream big, believe in yourself, and watch as the universe conspires to bring your desires to fruition.

Harnessing Mindset and Belief Systems for Manifestation

In the journey of manifestation, the role of mindset and belief systems is paramount. Our thoughts, beliefs, and attitudes not only shape our perception of reality but also influence our ability to attract abundance and manifest our desires. In this article, we will explore the profound impact of mindset and belief systems on the manifestation process, discussing how they shape our reality, affect our ability to attract abundance, and offering strategies for shifting limiting beliefs to align with our desires. Additionally, we will delve into the concept of vibrational alignment and how maintaining a positive mindset contributes to successful manifestation.

Our mindset and belief systems act as the lens through which we perceive the world around us. They are the filters that shape our thoughts, emotions, and actions, ultimately determining the outcomes we experience in life. When we hold empowering beliefs and maintain a positive mindset, we are more likely to attract positive experiences and opportunities into our lives. Conversely, when we harbor limiting beliefs and negative thought patterns, we create barriers to manifestation and hinder our ability to achieve our goals.

Beliefs are deeply ingrained assumptions about ourselves, others, and the world around us. They are formed through our experiences, upbringing, cultural influences, and societal conditioning. Our beliefs act as self-fulfilling prophecies, shaping our thoughts, emotions, and behaviors in alignment with our underlying assumptions. For example, if we believe that we are unworthy of success or abundance, we will unconsciously sabotage our efforts and repel opportunities that come our way.

Our mindset plays a crucial role in the manifestation process. A positive mindset is characterized by optimism, resilience, and a belief in one's ability to create positive change. When we cultivate a positive mindset, we open ourselves up to possibilities and opportunities, allowing us to envision and manifest our desires with greater ease and effectiveness. Conversely, a negative mindset, characterized by pessimism, self-doubt, and fear, creates resistance and blocks the flow of abundance into our lives.

Shifting limiting beliefs is a crucial step in the manifestation process. By identifying and challenging our limiting beliefs, we can create new neural pathways and rewire our brains for success. One effective strategy for shifting limiting beliefs is through cognitive reframing, which involves questioning the validity of negative beliefs and replacing them with more empowering alternatives. Affirmations, visualization, and hypnosis are also powerful tools for reprogramming the subconscious mind and instilling new, positive beliefs.

Vibrational alignment is the process of aligning our thoughts, emotions, and beliefs with the frequency of our desires. When we are in vibrational alignment with our desires, we emit a powerful energetic signal that attracts similar experiences and opportunities into our lives. Maintaining a positive mindset, practicing gratitude, and cultivating a sense of joy and abundance are all ways to raise our vibrational frequency and align ourselves with the manifestations we seek.

In conclusion, the role of mindset and belief systems in the manifestation process cannot be overstated. Our beliefs shape our reality, and our mindset determines our ability to attract abundance and manifest our desires. By cultivating a positive mindset, shifting limiting beliefs, and aligning ourselves with the frequency of our desires, we can harness the power within us to create the life of our dreams. So, dare to dream big, believe in yourself, and watch as the universe conspires to bring your desires to fruition.

Chapter 2: Setting Clear Intentions

In the previous chapter, we explored the foundational principles of the Law of Attraction and how our thoughts and beliefs shape our reality. Now, we delve deeper into the manifestation process by focusing on the crucial step of setting clear intentions.

Intentions act as the guiding force behind manifestation, directing our energy and attention towards our desired outcomes. When we set clear intentions, we provide the universe with a clear roadmap of what we want to attract into our lives. However, setting intentions goes beyond simply stating what we desire; it requires clarity, specificity, and alignment with our true desires and values.

In this chapter, we will uncover the importance of clarity in manifestation and explore practical strategies for identifying and setting clear intentions. We will discuss the process of identifying our desires, creating affirmations, vision boards, and aligning our actions with our intentions. By mastering the art of setting clear intentions, you will empower yourself to manifest your dreams with greater clarity, focus, and effectiveness.

Join us as we embark on this transformative journey of setting clear intentions and unlocking the power within to manifest the life you desire.

The Role of Clarity in Manifestation

In the journey of manifestation, clarity acts as the guiding beacon that illuminates our path towards realizing our desires. Without clarity, our intentions become muddled, our energy scattered, and our manifestations diluted. In this article, we delve into the importance of clarity in the manifestation process, exploring how it helps focus our energy, eliminates ambiguity, enhances effectiveness, and offering practical tips for achieving clarity in our intentions.

Clarity serves as the cornerstone of successful manifestation, providing a clear roadmap for the universe to follow in bringing our desires to fruition. When we possess clarity in our intentions, we send a strong and coherent signal to the universe, making it easier for it to respond and align with our desires. Without clarity, our energy becomes diffuse, and our manifestations lack the precision necessary for successful realization.

Vague or unclear intentions act as barriers to manifestation, creating mixed signals and hindering the manifestation process. When our intentions are ambiguous, the universe struggles to decipher our true desires, leading to confusion and delay in the manifestation of our goals. By eliminating ambiguity and getting crystal clear on what we want to manifest, we remove obstacles and pave the way for smoother manifestation outcomes.

Clarity significantly enhances the effectiveness of manifestation techniques such as visualization and affirmation. Clear intentions provide a precise target for the subconscious mind and the universe to focus on, amplifying the power of our thoughts and intentions. When we visualize or affirm with clarity, we reinforce our desires with unwavering certainty, signaling to the universe our unwavering commitment to their realization.

Achieving clarity in our intentions requires deliberate and focused effort. Practical strategies such as journaling, meditation, and visualization exercises can help clarify our desires and align our energy with our intentions. Journaling allows us to explore our desires in-depth, uncovering hidden motivations and values. Meditation provides a space for quiet reflection, allowing us to connect with our inner wisdom and intuition. Visualization exercises enable us to vividly imagine our desired outcomes, imbuing them with emotional resonance and clarity.

Practical Applications of Clarity:

Beyond its theoretical importance, clarity in manifestation has tangible practical applications that can significantly impact our everyday lives. When we possess clarity in our intentions, we make better decisions aligned with our goals, leading to more fulfilling outcomes in various aspects of life such as relationships, career, health, and personal growth.

1. Relationships:

Clarity in relationships allows us to establish clear boundaries, communicate effectively, and attract healthy connections into our lives. When we are clear about what we desire in a relationship, we become more discerning about the people we allow into our inner circle, leading to more meaningful and fulfilling connections.

2. Career:

In the realm of career and professional development, clarity enables us to set clear goals, make strategic decisions, and pursue opportunities aligned with our passions and values. When we have clarity about our career aspirations, we can focus our energy and efforts on activities that move us closer to our desired outcomes, leading to greater success and fulfillment in our professional endeavors.

3. Health:

Clarity in health and wellness empowers us to make informed choices that support our physical, mental, and emotional well-being. When we have clarity about our health goals and priorities, we can adopt healthier habits, seek appropriate support, and make proactive choices that contribute to our overall vitality and longevity.

4. Personal Growth:

Clarity in personal growth and self-development guides us on a journey of self-discovery, self-awareness, and self-improvement. When we are clear about our values, beliefs, and aspirations, we can align our actions with our highest potential, cultivate resilience, and overcome obstacles that hinder our growth and evolution.

Cultivating Clarity:

Cultivating clarity in our intentions is an ongoing process that requires dedication, self-reflection, and conscious effort. Here are some additional practical tips for nurturing clarity in our manifestation practice:

> **Visualization Practices:** Engage in regular visualization exercises where you vividly imagine yourself living your desired reality. Visualization helps clarify your intentions and imbues them with emotional resonance, making them more compelling and tangible.

> **Mindfulness Techniques:** Practice mindfulness techniques such as meditation, deep breathing, or mindfulness-based stress reduction to quiet the mind,

increase self-awareness, and connect with your inner guidance. Mindfulness cultivates clarity by helping you tune into your intuition and discern your true desires.

Goal Setting: Set SMART (Specific, Measurable, Achievable, Relevant, Time-bound) goals that are clear, concise, and actionable. Break down larger goals into smaller, manageable tasks, and create a plan of action to guide your efforts towards manifestation.

Journaling: Keep a manifestation journal where you record your intentions, progress, and insights. Journaling allows you to clarify your thoughts, identify patterns, and track your manifestation journey over time.

By incorporating these practical applications and cultivating clarity in our intentions, we can harness the transformative power of manifestation to create the life we desire. With clarity as our compass, we navigate the manifestation process with confidence, purpose, and unwavering determination, knowing that our intentions are clear and our dreams within reach.

Clarity is not merely a luxury but a necessity in the manifestation process. By cultivating clarity in our intentions, we empower ourselves to focus our energy, eliminate ambiguity, and enhance the effectiveness of our manifestation efforts. Through practical strategies and unwavering commitment, we can achieve the clarity necessary to manifest our deepest desires and create the life we envision. So, dare to get clear, dare to dream big, and watch as the universe aligns with your intentions to bring your desires to fruition.

The Path to Manifestation Mastery

In the pursuit of manifesting our dreams and desires, one crucial step often overlooked is the process of identifying what we truly want. Our desires serve as the compass guiding us towards our desired outcomes, yet many of us struggle to pinpoint exactly what it is that we long for. In this article, we embark on a journey of self-discovery and introspection, exploring the importance of identifying our desires, prioritizing them, honoring authenticity, and overcoming limiting beliefs that may hinder our manifestation efforts.

Self-awareness is the cornerstone of identifying our desires. It requires us to turn inward and explore our inner landscape, uncovering our values, passions, and goals. By cultivating self-awareness, we gain clarity on what truly matters to us, allowing us to set intentions that are aligned with our authentic selves.

To identify our desires, we must first understand what drives us and what brings us joy. Reflecting on our core values, passions, and long-term goals provides valuable insights into what we truly want to manifest in our lives. Take the time to journal, meditate, or engage in introspective exercises to uncover the desires that lie beneath the surface.

Not all desires are created equal, and it's essential to prioritize them based on their importance and relevance to our lives. Focusing on the most meaningful desires increases the likelihood of successful manifestation and ensures that our energy is directed towards that which truly matters to us. Take stock of your desires and rank them based on their significance in shaping your ideal life.

Authenticity is key to manifestation. Our true desires resonate deeply with our soul and are more likely to manifest when aligned with our authentic selves. Resist the urge to conform to societal expectations or external pressures, and instead honor your unique desires, no matter how unconventional they may seem. Embrace your authenticity, and watch as your desires effortlessly manifest into reality.

Limiting beliefs are the silent saboteurs that can derail our manifestation efforts. Addressing common barriers such as fear, self-doubt, and negative self-talk is essential in uncovering hidden desires and unlocking our full manifestation potential. Challenge these limiting beliefs by reframing negative thoughts, practicing self-compassion, and cultivating a growth mindset that empowers you to pursue your dreams fearlessly.

Identifying your desires is a transformative journey of self-discovery and empowerment. By cultivating self-awareness, prioritizing desires, honoring authenticity, and overcoming limiting beliefs, you pave the way for successful manifestation and the realization of your deepest desires. Embrace the journey with an open heart and a curious mind, and trust that the universe will conspire to bring your desires to fruition. Dare to dream big, and watch as your desires manifest into the vibrant reality you've always envisioned.

Creating Affirmations and Vision Boards:

Affirmations and vision boards are powerful tools in the manifestation process, serving as tangible reminders of our desires and aspirations. In this section, we'll explore how affirmations work to reprogram the subconscious mind and how vision boards help reinforce intentions through visual representation.

Affirmations: Reprogramming the Subconscious Mind

Affirmations are positive statements that affirm desired outcomes and beliefs, serving as powerful tools to reprogram the subconscious mind. By repeating affirmations consistently, we can overwrite negative thought patterns and beliefs, replacing them with positive affirmations that support our manifestation goals.

Tips for Creating Powerful Affirmations:

Be Specific: Ensure that your affirmations are specific and clearly define what you want to manifest. For example, instead of saying "I want to be successful," say "I am attracting success and abundance into my life."

Be Positive: Phrase your affirmations in a positive way, focusing on what you want to achieve rather than what you want to avoid. For instance, instead of saying "I am not afraid of failure," say "I am confident in my ability to succeed."

Use Present Tense: Frame your affirmations in the present tense as if your desired outcome has already manifested. This helps to create a sense of immediacy and reinforces the belief that your desires are within reach. For example, say "I am grateful for the abundance flowing into my life now."

Personalize Your Affirmations: Tailor your affirmations to resonate with your individual desires, beliefs, and values. Use language that feels authentic and meaningful to you, ensuring that your affirmations align with your innermost desires and aspirations.

Vision Boards: Bringing Intentions to Life

Vision boards are visual representations of our desired outcomes and experiences, serving as powerful tools to reinforce intentions through imagery. By creating a vision board, we externalize our desires and aspirations, making them tangible and accessible.

How Vision Boards Help Reinforce Intentions:

Visual Representation: Vision boards provide a visual representation of our goals and aspirations, making them more tangible and concrete. By seeing our desires manifested in images, we activate our imagination and strengthen our belief in their attainment.

Tangible Reminder: Placing our vision board in a prominent location serves as a constant reminder of our intentions. Every time we look at our vision board, we reinforce our commitment to manifesting our desires and align our energy with our goals.

Step-by-Step Guide to Creating a Vision Board:

Gather Supplies: Collect magazines, images, quotes, and other materials that resonate with your desires and aspirations.

Set Intentions: Clarify your intentions and goals for your vision board. What do you want to manifest in your life? What experiences do you want to attract?

Select Images: Choose images that represent your desires and aspirations. Look for visuals that evoke positive emotions and resonate with your vision.

Arrange Creatively: Arrange your selected images and materials on a poster board or canvas in a creative and visually appealing way. Allow your intuition to guide you as you arrange your vision board.

Display Prominently: Once complete, display your vision board in a prominent location where you will see it daily. This could be in your bedroom, office, or any other space where you spend time.

Engage with Your Vision Board: Take time each day to visualize yourself living your desired reality while engaging with your vision board. Imagine yourself experiencing the emotions and sensations of achieving your goals, and allow yourself to bask in the joy and fulfillment of manifesting your desires.

By incorporating affirmations and vision boards into your manifestation practice, you amplify the power of your intentions and create a visual roadmap to your desired reality. Embrace these tools as powerful allies on your journey of manifestation, and watch as your dreams effortlessly manifest into reality.

Unlocking the Power of Aligned Action: A Key to Manifestation Mastery

In the journey of manifestation, thoughts and beliefs serve as the foundation upon which our desires are built. However, without action, these intentions remain dormant potentials waiting to be realized. Aligned action bridges the gap between intention and manifestation, propelling us towards our goals with purpose and determination. In this article, we delve into the concept of aligned action, its significance in the manifestation process, and practical strategies for taking proactive steps towards realizing our dreams.

Aligned action refers to the proactive steps taken in harmony with our intentions and desires. It is the deliberate choice to engage in activities that move us closer to manifesting our goals. Unlike random or scattered actions, aligned action is purposeful and intentional, guided by our innermost desires and values.

While thoughts and beliefs lay the groundwork for manifestation, taking tangible steps towards our desires reinforces our commitment and signals to the universe our readiness to receive. Aligned action bridges the gap between the realm of imagination and the physical world, turning our dreams into tangible reality.

To effectively harness the power of aligned action, it's essential to break down our intentions into smaller, actionable steps. Large goals can feel overwhelming, but by dissecting them into manageable tasks, we make them more achievable and less daunting. Begin by brainstorming potential strategies, researching relevant resources, and seeking guidance from mentors or experts to identify specific actions that align with each intention.

A structured action plan serves as a roadmap to guide our efforts towards manifesting our goals. By creating a well-defined plan, we maintain focus and accountability, ensuring that we stay on track despite obstacles or distractions. Strive for a balance between flexibility and structure in your action plan. Flexibility allows for adjustments and adaptations as circumstances change, while structure provides a framework for progress and accountability.

Consistency is key in taking aligned action. Regular, consistent effort compounds over time and increases the likelihood of manifestation. Cultivate discipline by setting specific goals, establishing routines, and practicing self-discipline techniques such as time management and prioritization. Stay committed to your action plan, even when faced with challenges or setbacks, and trust in the process of manifestation.

Resistance and procrastination are common barriers to taking aligned action. Explore the root causes of resistance, such as fear, self-doubt, or limiting beliefs, and develop strategies for overcoming them. Break tasks into smaller, more manageable chunks, reward yourself for progress, and seek support from accountability partners or coaches to stay motivated and on track.

Celebrate your achievements and milestones along the way to reinforce positive momentum and motivation. Periodically review and adjust your action plan as needed, based on feedback and results. Manifestation is a dynamic process, and it's essential to adapt your approach to align with your evolving goals and desires.

Aligned action is the catalyst that transforms intentions into reality. By taking proactive steps towards our desires, we demonstrate our commitment to manifestation and invite the universe to conspire in our favor. Embrace the power of aligned action, cultivate consistency and discipline, and celebrate your progress along the way. With focused effort and unwavering determination, you can manifest your deepest desires and create the life you envision.

The Power of Focus and Persistence in Manifestation

In the pursuit of our dreams and desires, maintaining focus and persistence is akin to tending a flame—it requires constant attention, nurturing, and unwavering commitment. In the manifestation journey, where thoughts shape reality and intentions pave the way for manifestation, staying steadfast in our resolve becomes paramount. In this article, we explore the significance of maintaining focus and persistence, the challenges that arise amidst distractions and setbacks, and practical strategies for cultivating resilience and perseverance along the manifestation path.

In the vast sea of possibilities, focus acts as our guiding light, illuminating the path towards our desired outcomes. Without it, we risk drifting aimlessly, unable to discern the next steps towards manifestation. Persistence, on the other hand, fuels our journey, propelling us forward in the face of obstacles and challenges. Together, focus and persistence form the backbone of successful manifestation, turning dreams into tangible reality.

In today's fast-paced world, distractions abound at every turn, pulling us away from our intentions and diluting our focus. Whether it's the constant barrage of notifications, external pressures, or inner doubts and fears, maintaining clarity amidst the noise can be a daunting task. Moreover, setbacks and obstacles are inevitable on the manifestation journey, testing our resolve and tempting us to abandon our goals. In the face of these challenges, it's easy to lose sight of our intentions and succumb to inertia.

Practical Tips for Cultivating Resilience and Perseverance:

Clarify Your Vision: Begin by clarifying your vision and intentions. Define what you want to manifest with clarity and specificity, and keep your vision at the forefront of your mind. Visualize your desired outcomes regularly, imbuing them with emotion and conviction.

Set Clear Goals: Break down your intentions into smaller, actionable goals. Setting clear, achievable milestones allows you to track your progress and stay motivated along the way. Celebrate each milestone as you move closer to your ultimate vision.

Create a Sacred Space: Designate a quiet, clutter-free space where you can immerse yourself in manifestation practices without distractions. Whether it's a cozy corner of your home or a serene outdoor retreat, having a sacred space dedicated to your manifestation rituals can enhance focus and concentration.

Practice Mindfulness: Cultivate mindfulness through meditation, deep breathing exercises, or mindful awareness throughout your day. Mindfulness helps anchor your attention in the present moment, reducing stress and anxiety while fostering clarity and concentration.

Stay Flexible Yet Persistent: While maintaining focus is crucial, it's also essential to remain flexible in your approach. Be willing to adapt and adjust your strategies as needed, but never waver in your commitment to your goals. Persistence is the fuel that propels you forward, even when the path seems uncertain or challenging.

Seek Support and Accountability: Surround yourself with supportive individuals who believe in your vision and encourage your growth. Share your goals with trusted friends, mentors, or coaches who can offer guidance, accountability, and motivation during times of doubt or uncertainty.

Practice Self-Compassion: Be gentle with yourself on the journey. Acknowledge that setbacks and challenges are a natural part of the manifestation process and offer yourself kindness and compassion during difficult times. Treat yourself with the same level of care and understanding that you would extend to a dear friend facing similar challenges.

Maintaining focus and persistence is not merely a virtue but a necessity on the manifestation journey. By nurturing our focus and cultivating resilience, we harness the power within us to overcome obstacles, navigate challenges, and manifest our deepest desires. With unwavering determination and a steadfast commitment to our goals, we can illuminate the path ahead and bring our dreams into tangible reality. Remember, the flame of manifestation burns brightest in the hearts of those who dare to persist in the face of adversity.

Chapter 3: Cultivating a Positive Mindset

In the vast landscape of human experience, our mindset serves as the lens through which we perceive and interpret the world around us. It shapes our thoughts, influences our emotions, and ultimately determines the trajectory of our lives. At the heart of this intricate web of cognition and perception lies the concept of a positive mindset—a transformative state of being characterized by optimism, resilience, and an unwavering belief in the inherent goodness of life.

In this chapter, we delve deep into the profound significance of cultivating a positive mindset through our exploration into manifestation and abundance. Just as a gardener tends to the soil to nurture the growth of vibrant blooms, so too must we develop the fertile ground of our minds to foster the blossoming of positivity, optimism, and abundance in our lives.

Positivity is more than just a fleeting emotion or fleeting moment of joy; it is a fundamental state of being that colors our perception of reality. When we approach life with a positive mindset, we are better equipped to navigate challenges, overcome obstacles, and seize opportunities with courage and conviction. Positivity fuels our resilience, propelling us forward even in the face of adversity, and illuminates the path towards our dreams with unwavering clarity.

Our beliefs and thoughts serve as the building blocks of our mindset, shaping our perceptions and influencing our behavior. Negative beliefs and thought patterns can act as barriers to our happiness and success, clouding our vision and limiting our potential. By identifying and challenging these negative beliefs, we can begin to shift our mindset towards one of positivity and empowerment, opening ourselves up to a world of limitless possibilities.

At the heart of a positive mindset lies the practice of gratitude and appreciation. When we cultivate an attitude of gratitude, we shift our focus from what is lacking to what is abundant in our lives. Gratitude serves as a powerful antidote to negativity, fostering feelings of joy, contentment, and inner peace. By practicing gratitude daily, we train our minds to seek out the beauty and goodness in every moment, no matter how small or seemingly insignificant.

Optimism is the fuel that propels us forward on our journey towards manifestation and abundance. When we approach life with optimism, we see challenges as opportunities for growth, setbacks as temporary detours on the road to success, and failures as valuable lessons to be learned. Optimism breeds resilience, enabling us to bounce back from adversity with renewed strength and determination, and to continue moving forward towards our goals with unwavering faith in our abilities.

In a world filled with distractions and noise, mindfulness offers a refuge of peace and tranquility amidst the chaos. By practicing present-moment awareness, we learn to quiet the chatter of our minds and connect with the richness of life unfolding around us. Mindfulness fosters a deeper appreciation for the beauty and wonder of the present moment, grounding us in a sense of gratitude and awe for the miracle of existence.

As we embark on this journey of cultivating a positive mindset, may we embrace the transformative power of positivity, optimism, and gratitude. May we nourish the soil of our minds with love, kindness, and compassion, and may we witness the abundant fruits of our labor as we manifest our deepest desires and dreams into reality.

Harnessing the Power of Positivity: A Pathway to Resilience and Well-being

In human experience, positivity emerges as a radiant thread, weaving its way through the fabric of our thoughts, emotions, and actions. It is a transformative force—a beacon of light that illuminates the darkest of days and infuses our lives with hope, resilience, and joy. In this article, we embark on a journey to explore the profound impact of positivity on our well-being, delving into its essence, unraveling its mysteries, and uncovering the myriad ways in which it shapes our lives.

At its core, positivity is more than just a fleeting emotion or passing fancy; it is a state of mind—a way of being—that colors our perception of the world around us. It is the lens through which we view life, imbuing even the most mundane moments with a sense of wonder and possibility. Positivity is the gentle whisper of encouragement that lifts our spirits when we falter, the guiding light that leads us through the darkest of nights, and the unwavering belief that tomorrow holds the promise of brighter days.

The ripple effects of positivity extend far beyond the confines of our minds, permeating every aspect of our being. In our thoughts, positivity acts as a catalyst for creativity and innovation, sparking new ideas and inspiring bold action. It imbues our emotions with warmth and vitality, infusing even the most challenging situations with a sense of peace and serenity. And in our actions, positivity serves as a guiding force, propelling us forward with purpose and conviction, and empowering us to overcome obstacles with grace and dignity.

One of the most remarkable qualities of positivity is its ability to foster resilience in the face of adversity. When we approach life with a positive mindset, we are better equipped to weather the storms that inevitably come our way. Rather than succumbing to despair or hopelessness, we rise above our challenges with courage and determination, knowing that every setback is merely a stepping stone on the path to growth and transformation. Positivity fuels our resilience, enabling us to bounce back from adversity with renewed strength and vitality, and to emerge from even the darkest of times with a newfound sense of purpose and clarity.

At its essence, positivity is the key to unlocking the door to happiness and overall well-being. When we cultivate a positive mindset, we open ourselves up to a world of abundance and possibility, where every moment is infused with joy and gratitude. Positivity enhances our relationships, deepens our connections with others, and fosters a sense of belonging and community. It nourishes our souls, replenishing our spirits with hope and optimism, and guiding us towards a life filled with purpose, meaning, and fulfillment.

While positivity may seem elusive at times, it is a quality that can be nurtured and cultivated through mindful practice and intention. Here are some practical tips for cultivating positivity in your life:

> **Practice Gratitude:** Take time each day to reflect on the things you are grateful for, no matter how small or seemingly insignificant. Cultivating an attitude of gratitude helps shift your focus from what is lacking to what is abundant in your life.

Surround Yourself with Positivity: Surround yourself with people, places, and experiences that uplift and inspire you. Seek out positive influences and environments that foster joy, laughter, and growth.

Focus on Solutions: Instead of dwelling on problems or setbacks, focus your energy on finding solutions and taking proactive steps towards resolution. Positivity thrives in an environment of optimism and possibility.

Practice Self-Compassion: Be kind and gentle with yourself, especially during times of difficulty or struggle. Treat yourself with the same level of compassion and understanding that you would extend to a dear friend facing similar challenges.

Engage in Activities that Bring You Joy: Take time each day to engage in activities that bring you joy and fulfillment, whether it's spending time in nature, pursuing a creative passion, or connecting with loved ones. Cultivating moments of joy and happiness nourishes your soul and strengthens your positive mindset.

In a world filled with uncertainty and turmoil, positivity stands as a beacon of hope—a guiding light that leads us towards a brighter, more hopeful future. By cultivating a positive mindset, we unlock the door to resilience, happiness, and overall well-being, and embark on a journey of self-discovery and transformation. May we embrace the power of positivity in our lives, and may its radiant light shine brightly within us, guiding us towards a life filled with love, joy, and abundance.

Shaping Your Reality: The Power of Beliefs and Thoughts

In the intricate of human consciousness, our beliefs and thoughts serve as the threads that weave together the fabric of our reality. From the moment we wake until we drift into slumber, our minds are filled with a constant stream of thoughts, beliefs, and perceptions that shape our experiences and influence our actions. In this article, we delve into the profound role of beliefs and thoughts in shaping our mindset, and explore how identifying and challenging negative beliefs can lead to a more positive outlook on life.

Our beliefs and thoughts act as the lenses through which we perceive the world around us. They color our interpretation of events, shape our emotions, and ultimately determine the quality of our experiences. Positive beliefs and thoughts foster a mindset of optimism, resilience, and empowerment, while negative beliefs can give rise to feelings of doubt, fear, and limitation. By understanding the influence of our beliefs and thoughts on our mindset, we gain insight into the profound impact they have on our lives.

Negative beliefs lurk beneath the surface of our consciousness, subtly influencing our perceptions and behaviors. They stem from past experiences, societal conditioning, and ingrained patterns of thought, often operating at a subconscious level. Identifying negative beliefs is the first step towards cultivating a more positive outlook on life. By shining a light on these hidden beliefs, we become aware of the ways in which they shape our reality and can begin to challenge their validity.

Challenging negative beliefs requires courage, introspection, and a willingness to question the stories we tell ourselves. It involves examining the evidence supporting these beliefs, exploring alternative perspectives, and reframing our thoughts in a more positive light. By challenging negative beliefs, we open ourselves up to new possibilities and pave the way for a more optimistic and empowered mindset.

Practical Tips for Identifying and Challenging Negative Beliefs

> **Self-Reflection:** Take time to reflect on your beliefs and thoughts, paying attention to recurring patterns or themes. Notice when negative thoughts arise and examine the underlying beliefs driving them.

> **Question Assumptions:** Challenge the validity of negative beliefs by asking yourself questions such as "Is this belief based on fact or perception?" "What evidence do I have to support this belief?" and "How does this belief serve me?"

> **Seek Contrary Evidence:** Look for evidence that contradicts negative beliefs, challenging their accuracy and validity. This could involve seeking out alternative

perspectives, gathering information, or engaging in self-experimentation.

Practice Affirmations: Counteract negative beliefs with positive affirmations that reinforce empowering beliefs. Repeat affirmations daily to reprogram your subconscious mind and cultivate a more positive mindset.

Visualize Success: Use visualization techniques to imagine yourself achieving your goals and overcoming obstacles. Visualization helps to rewire the brain, making it easier to challenge negative beliefs and cultivate a more positive outlook on life.

Our beliefs and thoughts are powerful tools that shape our perception of reality and influence the quality of our lives. By identifying and challenging negative beliefs, we can cultivate a more positive mindset that empowers us to overcome obstacles, pursue our goals, and live a life filled with joy, purpose, and fulfillment. May we harness the power of our beliefs and thoughts to shape a reality that aligns with our deepest desires and aspirations.

Embracing Gratitude: A Pathway to a Positive Mindset

In a world filled with hustle and bustle, it's easy to lose sight of the simple joys and blessings that surround us each day. Yet, amidst the chaos of modern life, lies a powerful antidote to negativity and stress: gratitude. The practice of gratitude and appreciation has the remarkable ability to transform our mindset, fostering feelings of joy, contentment, and inner peace. In this article, we delve into the profound benefits of practicing gratitude and offer practical tips and exercises for incorporating gratitude practices into daily life.

Gratitude is more than just a fleeting emotion or polite gesture; it is a way of life—a conscious choice to focus on the abundance and blessings that exist in every moment. When we cultivate an attitude of gratitude, we shift our perspective from what is lacking to what is present, from what went wrong to what went right, and from despair to hope. Gratitude opens our hearts to the beauty and wonder of life, infusing even the most ordinary moments with a sense of wonder and appreciation.

Benefits of Practicing Gratitude

Enhanced Well-being: Numerous studies have shown that practicing gratitude is associated with greater levels of happiness, life satisfaction, and overall well-being. By focusing on the positive aspects of life, we train our brains to notice and appreciate the good, leading to a more optimistic outlook on life.

Improved Relationships: Expressing gratitude towards others fosters deeper connections and strengthens relationships. Gratitude cultivates feelings of warmth, kindness, and generosity, enhancing the quality of our interactions and fostering a sense of mutual appreciation and respect.

Reduced Stress: Gratitude acts as a natural stress reliever, helping to counteract the negative effects of stress on the body and mind. By shifting our focus from worries and anxieties to blessings and abundance, we activate the body's relaxation response, promoting feelings of calm and tranquility.

Increased Resilience: Practicing gratitude enhances our ability to bounce back from adversity and overcome challenges with grace and resilience. By acknowledging the silver linings in difficult situations, we cultivate a sense of hope and optimism that empowers us to persevere in the face of obstacles.

Practical Tips for Incorporating Gratitude Practices

Keep a Gratitude Journal: Set aside a few minutes each day to write down three things you are grateful for. Focus on specific moments, experiences, or people that have brought joy or meaning to your life. Reflect on why you are grateful for each blessing and savor the positive emotions that arise.

Practice Mindful Gratitude: Incorporate gratitude into your daily mindfulness practice by taking moments throughout the day to pause and reflect on what you are grateful for. Use your senses to anchor yourself in the present moment and notice the beauty and abundance that surrounds you.

Express Gratitude to Others: Take time to express gratitude to the people in your life who have positively impacted you. Write a heartfelt thank-you note, send a text or email expressing your appreciation, or verbally express your gratitude in person. Acts of gratitude not only uplift others but also deepen your own sense of connection and fulfillment.

Create a Gratitude Ritual: Establish a daily or weekly gratitude ritual that allows you to cultivate feelings of appreciation and abundance. This could involve lighting a candle, saying a prayer of gratitude, or engaging in a gratitude meditation practice. Find a ritual that resonates with you and commit to practicing it consistently.

Shift Your Perspective: Challenge yourself to reframe negative situations or experiences in a more positive light by focusing on what you can learn or how you can grow from them. Look for the silver linings, lessons, or blessings hidden within challenging circumstances, and express gratitude for the growth opportunities they present.

In a world that often emphasizes what is lacking or imperfect, practicing gratitude offers a powerful antidote—a reminder to focus on the abundance and blessings that surround us each day. By incorporating gratitude practices into our daily lives, we cultivate a positive mindset that uplifts our spirits, strengthens our relationships, and enhances our overall well-being. May we embrace the transformative power of gratitude and appreciate the richness and beauty of life in all its forms.

Thriving Through Adversity: The Power of Optimism and Resilience

In human experience, optimism and resilience emerge as steadfast companions, guiding us through life's myriad challenges and triumphs. While optimism infuses our days with hope and possibility, resilience empowers us to bounce back from setbacks with grace and determination. In this article, we explore the intricate relationship between optimism, resilience, and a positive mindset, and offer strategies for fostering these qualities, even in the face of adversity.

The Interplay of Optimism, Resilience, and Positive Mindset

Optimism, resilience, and a positive mindset are deeply intertwined, each reinforcing and bolstering the other. Optimism serves as a beacon of light, illuminating the path ahead and infusing even the darkest moments with hope and possibility. It is the unwavering belief that challenges are temporary and setbacks are opportunities for growth. Resilience, on the other hand, is the inner strength and fortitude that enables us to weather life's storms with grace and courage. It is the ability to adapt, bounce back, and emerge stronger from adversity. Together, optimism and resilience form the foundation of a positive mindset—a mindset characterized by hope, perseverance, and an unwavering belief in the inherent goodness of life.

Strategies for Fostering Optimism

> **Practice Gratitude:** Cultivate an attitude of gratitude by regularly reflecting on the blessings and abundance in your life. Keep a gratitude journal, where you can jot down three things you are thankful for each day. Focusing on the positive aspects of life helps shift your perspective towards optimism.

> **Challenge Negative Thoughts:** Become aware of negative thought patterns and challenge them with more optimistic alternatives. Replace pessimistic thoughts with affirmations or positive affirmations that reinforce your belief in yourself and your ability to overcome challenges.

> **Visualize Success:** Use visualization techniques to imagine yourself succeeding in your goals and overcoming obstacles. Visualizing success not only boosts your confidence but also primes your mind for positive outcomes, making optimism more accessible.

> **Surround Yourself with Positivity:** Surround yourself with people, environments, and experiences that uplift and inspire you. Seek out positive influences and avoid dwelling on negativity or pessimism. Engage in activities that bring

you joy and fulfillment, and cultivate a supportive network of friends and loved ones who encourage and uplift you.

Focus on Solutions: Instead of dwelling on problems or setbacks, focus your energy on finding solutions and taking proactive steps towards resolution. Approach challenges with a can-do attitude and a belief in your ability to overcome obstacles. By focusing on solutions, you empower yourself to navigate difficulties with optimism and resilience.

Strategies for Cultivating Resilience

Develop a Growth Mindset: Embrace challenges as opportunities for growth and learning. Adopt a growth mindset, characterized by a belief in your ability to improve and develop through effort and perseverance. View setbacks as stepping stones on the path to success, rather than insurmountable obstacles.

Build a Strong Support Network: Cultivate relationships with friends, family, mentors, and peers who offer encouragement, support, and guidance. Lean on your support network during difficult times, and be willing to offer support to others in return. A strong support network provides a safety net during times of adversity and enhances your resilience.

Practice Self-Compassion: Be kind and gentle with yourself, especially during times of difficulty or struggle. Treat yourself with the same level of compassion and understanding that you would extend to a dear friend facing similar challenges. Practice self-care activities that nourish your body, mind, and spirit, and prioritize your well-being.

Foster Adaptability: Cultivate flexibility and adaptability in the face of change and uncertainty. Embrace change as a natural part of life and be willing to adjust your plans and expectations accordingly. Develop coping skills that help you navigate transitions with resilience and grace.

Maintain Perspective: Keep things in perspective by focusing on the bigger picture and recognizing that setbacks are temporary. Remind yourself of past challenges you have overcome and the lessons you have learned along the way. By maintaining perspective, you can weather difficulties with resilience and optimism.

In the midst of the complexities of human existence, optimism and resilience emerge as steadfast pillars, providing unwavering support through the myriad challenges and triumphs of life. Nurturing these qualities, particularly in the face of adversity, cultivates a positive mindset that propels us forward with confidence and vitality. Let's wholeheartedly embrace the transformative power of optimism and resilience, allowing them to illuminate our path towards personal growth, fulfillment, and well-being.

The Power of Mindfulness and Present-Moment Awareness

In the fast-paced modern world, the art of mindfulness offers a sanctuary—a refuge from the chaos and noise of everyday life. Rooted in ancient wisdom and timeless practices, mindfulness invites us to embrace the present moment with open-hearted awareness and curiosity. In this article, we explore the transformative power of mindfulness and present-moment awareness in cultivating a positive mindset, fostering gratitude, reducing stress, and enhancing overall well-being.

Mindfulness is more than just a passing trend; it is a way of being— a conscious choice to bring our attention and awareness to the present moment, without judgment or attachment. At its core, mindfulness involves cultivating a heightened sense of awareness and acceptance of our thoughts, feelings, sensations, and surroundings. By tuning into the present moment with curiosity and openness, we create space for clarity, insight, and inner peace to arise.

Present-moment awareness is the heart of mindfulness—a practice of being fully engaged and immersed in the here and now. It involves anchoring our attention to the sensations of our breath, the sights and sounds of our environment, and the sensations in our body. By grounding ourselves in the present moment, we release the grip of past regrets and future worries, allowing us to fully experience the richness and beauty of life as it unfolds.

Mindful awareness opens the door to gratitude—a profound sense of appreciation for the abundance and blessings that surround us each day. By slowing down and paying attention to the present moment, we become attuned to the simple joys and wonders of life that often go unnoticed. From the warmth of the sun on our skin to the laughter of loved ones, each moment becomes an opportunity for gratitude and appreciation.

In the midst of life's busyness and demands, mindfulness offers a reprieve—a sanctuary of calm amidst the storm. By cultivating present-moment awareness, we learn to step out of the cycle of stress and reactivity, and into a space of centeredness and ease. Mindfulness practices such as mindful breathing, body scans, and meditation serve as powerful tools for managing stress, promoting relaxation, and fostering emotional resilience.

Mindfulness is not just a practice; it is a way of life—a holistic approach to nurturing our physical, mental, and emotional well-being. Research has shown that regular mindfulness practice is associated with a myriad of benefits, including improved mood, enhanced cognitive function, and reduced symptoms of anxiety and depression. By prioritizing mindfulness in our daily lives, we empower ourselves to live with greater clarity, balance, and vitality.

Practical Tips for Cultivating Mindfulness and Present-Moment Awareness

Start Small: Begin by incorporating short mindfulness practices into your daily routine, such as mindful breathing exercises or brief moments of present-moment awareness throughout the day.

Practice Regularly: Consistency is key to reaping the benefits of mindfulness. Set aside dedicated time each day for formal mindfulness practice, such as meditation or yoga, and weave moments of mindfulness into your everyday activities.

Stay Curious: Approach mindfulness with a spirit of curiosity and openness. Allow yourself to explore different mindfulness practices and techniques, and notice how each one impacts your experience of the present moment.

Be Kind to Yourself: Mindfulness is a journey, not a destination. Be gentle and compassionate with yourself as you cultivate your practice, and remember that each moment is an opportunity to begin anew.

Find Support: Seek out community or resources to support your mindfulness journey, whether it's through joining a meditation group, attending a mindfulness retreat, or accessing online courses and guided meditations.

Mindfulness and present-moment awareness offer a pathway to greater presence, peace, and joy in our lives. By embracing the richness of the present moment with open-hearted awareness, we cultivate a positive mindset that nourishes our spirit and enhances our well-being. May we continue to journey inward, with mindfulness as our compass, guiding us towards a life of greater clarity, connection, and fulfillment.

Chapter 4: Manifesting Wealth and Financial Abundance

In the intricate of human existence, the pursuit of wealth and financial abundance occupies a central thread—a thread woven with dreams of prosperity, security, and fulfillment. Yet, for many, the journey towards financial abundance remains elusive, fraught with obstacles, doubts, and uncertainties. It is within this realm of aspiration and endeavor that the profound principles of manifestation offer a beacon of hope—a guiding light illuminating the path towards the realization of our deepest desires.

Chapter 4 of our journey delves into the realm of Manifesting Wealth and Financial Abundance—a chapter brimming with insights, strategies, and transformative practices aimed at harnessing the limitless potential of the universe to manifest material abundance and financial prosperity. As we embark on this exploration, we embark on a journey of self-discovery, empowerment, and liberation—a journey that transcends mere accumulation of wealth to embrace the true essence of abundance in all its forms.

At the heart of our quest for financial abundance lies the profound principle of attraction—the innate ability to draw forth from the universe that which we most fervently desire. Through the practice of manifestation techniques such as visualization, affirmations, and gratitude, we tap into the boundless reservoir of universal energy, aligning our thoughts, beliefs, and intentions with the frequency of wealth and prosperity. By cultivating a mindset of abundance and clarity of purpose, we pave the way for the effortless flow of financial abundance into our lives.

Central to our journey towards financial abundance is the cultivation of an abundance mindset—an unwavering belief in the infinite abundance of the universe and our inherent worthiness to receive its blessings. In contrast to the scarcity mindset, which operates from a place of fear, lack, and limitation, the abundance mindset is characterized by optimism, gratitude, and a profound sense of possibility. By shifting our perspective from scarcity to abundance, we open ourselves to the boundless opportunities and possibilities that surround us, allowing wealth and prosperity to flow effortlessly into our lives.

As we navigate the terrain of financial manifestation, it becomes imperative to translate our dreams and aspirations into tangible actions and strategies. From budgeting and saving to investing and wealth management, practical strategies serve as the bridge between our vision of financial abundance and its realization in the material world. By taking inspired action, aligning our behavior with our financial goals, and cultivating habits of discipline and resilience, we lay the groundwork for the manifestation of wealth and prosperity in our lives.

No journey towards financial abundance is without its challenges and setbacks. Yet, it is through adversity that we cultivate resilience, strength, and wisdom—the very qualities that propel us towards our goals with unwavering determination. By overcoming limiting beliefs, fears, and self-imposed barriers, we emerge stronger, more empowered, and more attuned to the infinite possibilities that lie before us. With resilience as our companion, we navigate the twists and turns of the financial journey with grace, courage, and unwavering faith in our ability to manifest our deepest desires.

As we embark on the voyage of manifesting wealth and financial abundance, we embark on a journey of transformation—a journey that transcends the realm of mere material acquisition to embrace the true essence of abundance in all its forms. With each step we take, we move closer to the realization of our dreams, our aspirations, and our highest potential. May this chapter serve as a guiding light—a beacon of hope and inspiration—as we unlock the boundless riches of the universe and step boldly into the realm of infinite possibility.

Unveiling the Secrets of Financial Manifestation: Attracting Money and Prosperity

In the realm of manifestation, the quest for financial abundance stands as a prominent aspiration for many—a pursuit fueled by dreams of prosperity, security, and freedom. Yet, for some, the path to wealth and financial success remains shrouded in mystery, elusive and unattainable. It is within this realm of possibility and potential that the profound principles of manifestation offer a beacon of hope—a gateway to unlocking the limitless abundance of the universe.

At the heart of financial manifestation lies the fundamental principle of attraction—the innate ability to draw forth from the universe that which we most fervently desire. Through the practice of manifestation techniques tailored specifically to financial abundance, individuals can harness the power of their thoughts, beliefs, and intentions to manifest wealth and prosperity into their lives.

Exploring Manifestation Methods: Tools for Financial Abundance

Various manifestation methods serve as potent tools for attracting money and prosperity, each offering unique pathways to financial abundance. Visualization, affirmations, scripting, and gratitude practices are among the most powerful techniques employed in the pursuit of wealth and financial success.

> Visualization: By vividly imagining oneself already in possession of the desired wealth and financial abundance, individuals can activate the subconscious mind to align with their intentions. Visualization techniques involve creating detailed mental images of financial goals achieved, thereby programming the mind for success.

> Affirmations: Affirmations are positive statements affirming desired outcomes and beliefs related to wealth and prosperity. By repeating affirmations regularly with conviction and belief, individuals can reprogram their subconscious mind to attract financial abundance into their lives.

> Scripting: Scripting involves the practice of writing down one's financial goals and intentions as if they have already been realized. Through the act of writing, individuals clarify their desires, reinforce their beliefs, and create a tangible roadmap for manifesting wealth and financial success.

> Gratitude Practices: Cultivating an attitude of gratitude is a powerful manifestation technique that shifts focus from scarcity to abundance. By expressing gratitude for existing blessings and anticipated abundance, individuals open themselves to receive the wealth and prosperity they seek.

When setting financial goals and intentions, clarity and specificity play pivotal roles in the manifestation process. Clearly defining financial objectives, specifying desired outcomes, and setting measurable targets provide focus and direction for manifestation efforts. By articulating financial goals with precision, individuals create a clear blueprint for the universe to follow, increasing the likelihood of successful manifestation.

Throughout history, countless individuals have effectively attracted wealth and financial abundance using manifestation principles. From entrepreneurs and business moguls to artists and visionaries, real-life success stories abound, showcasing the transformative power of manifestation in action. These stories serve as powerful inspiration and motivation for individuals seeking to manifest their own financial dreams, demonstrating that with faith, perseverance, and aligned action, anything is possible.

As we embark on the journey of attracting money and prosperity through manifestation, we step into a realm of infinite possibility— a realm where dreams become reality, and abundance flows effortlessly into our lives. By harnessing the power of attraction and utilizing manifestation techniques tailored to financial abundance, we empower ourselves to create the wealth and prosperity we desire.

Embracing Abundance: Unlocking the Power of the Abundance Mindset

In the intricate dance of life, our mindset serves as the lens through which we perceive the world—a lens that shapes our beliefs, influences our behaviors, and ultimately determines our destiny. At the heart of this mindset lies a fundamental dichotomy: the abundance mindset versus the scarcity mindset. These two contrasting perspectives hold immense power over our financial well-being, guiding our attitudes towards wealth, success, and abundance. In this article, we embark on a journey of exploration and transformation, delving into the depths of the abundance mindset and scarcity mindset, uncovering their profound effects on financial prosperity, and discovering practical strategies for cultivating an abundance mindset that attracts wealth and abundance into our lives.

The abundance mindset is characterized by a belief in the limitless possibilities of the universe—a belief that there is more than enough to go around and that opportunities for success and prosperity are abundant. In contrast, the scarcity mindset is rooted in fear and lack, operating from a place of scarcity and limitation—a belief that resources are scarce, opportunities are few, and success is reserved for the select few.

The abundance mindset is marked by qualities such as optimism, gratitude, and a sense of abundance in all areas of life. Those who embody this mindset approach challenges with resilience, view setbacks as opportunities for growth, and attract abundance effortlessly into their lives. On the other hand, individuals with a scarcity mindset tend to focus on what they lack, dwell on limitations, and operate from a place of fear and insecurity. This mindset can lead to feelings of anxiety, stress, and dissatisfaction, ultimately sabotaging one's ability to attract and manage wealth.

The abundance mindset is rooted in beliefs about abundance, worthiness, and self-esteem. Those who possess this mindset believe they are deserving of success and abundance and trust in their ability to create the life they desire. In contrast, the scarcity mindset is driven by fears of inadequacy, unworthiness, and a deep-seated belief that there is not enough to go around. These beliefs are often formed in childhood based on past experiences, societal conditioning, and cultural influences.

Our mindset profoundly influences our behavior and decision-making, shaping the actions we take and the outcomes we experience. Those with an abundance mindset approach life with a sense of possibility and optimism, taking calculated risks, seizing opportunities, and investing in their own growth and development. In contrast, individuals with a scarcity mindset tend to operate from a place of fear and limitation, avoiding risk-taking, hoarding resources, and holding back from pursuing their goals and dreams.

Shifting from a scarcity mindset to an abundance mindset requires conscious effort and practice. Here are some practical exercises and strategies to help cultivate an abundance mindset:

> Reframe Negative Thoughts: Challenge negative beliefs and thoughts about scarcity by reframing them into positive

affirmations of abundance and possibility. Replace thoughts of lack with thoughts of abundance and gratitude.

Practice Gratitude: Cultivate an attitude of gratitude by focusing on the blessings and abundance already present in your life. Keep a gratitude journal, regularly reflecting on what you are thankful for, and expressing appreciation for the abundance around you.

Focus on Abundance in All Areas of Life: Expand your perspective beyond financial wealth and abundance to encompass all areas of life, including health, relationships, and personal growth. Recognize and celebrate abundance in all its forms.

Set Clear Goals and Intentions: Define your financial goals and intentions with clarity and specificity. Visualize yourself achieving these goals and focus your energy and attention on manifesting them into reality.

Surround Yourself with Abundance: Surround yourself with people, environments, and experiences that embody abundance and success. Seek out mentors, role models, and communities that inspire and uplift you on your journey towards abundance.

As we conclude our exploration of the abundance mindset versus the scarcity mindset, we are reminded of the profound influence our mindset has on our financial well-being and overall quality of life. By cultivating an abundance mindset rooted in optimism, gratitude, and possibility, we unlock the power to attract wealth, success, and abundance into our lives. May this article serve as a beacon of inspiration and empowerment, guiding you on your journey towards financial prosperity and fulfillment.

Mastering Financial Manifestation: Practical Strategies for Abundance and Success

In the pursuit of financial abundance and success, the art of manifestation serves as a powerful ally—an invaluable tool for transforming dreams into reality and aspirations into achievements. Yet, amidst the vast landscape of financial manifestation, practicality and action are paramount, guiding our efforts towards tangible results and sustainable wealth. In this article, we embark on a journey of exploration and empowerment, uncovering practical strategies for manifesting financial abundance in everyday life. From budgeting and saving to investing and overcoming obstacles, let us delve into the depths of financial manifestation and discover the keys to unlocking lasting prosperity and abundance.

At the core of financial manifestation lies the principle of inspired action—the conscious choice to align our behavior with our financial goals and intentions. Taking inspired action involves stepping out of our comfort zones, seizing opportunities, and making intentional decisions that propel us towards our desired outcomes. By aligning our actions with our financial aspirations, we harness the power of manifestation to attract wealth, abundance, and success into our lives.

Budgeting and saving serve as the cornerstones of financial manifestation, providing a solid foundation upon which to build wealth and prosperity. By creating a budget that aligns with our financial goals and priorities, we gain clarity and control over our finances, allowing us to allocate resources strategically and eliminate unnecessary expenses. Similarly, practicing disciplined saving habits enables us to accumulate wealth gradually over time, setting the stage for long-term financial abundance and security.

Investing represents a key strategy for multiplying wealth and achieving financial abundance. Whether through stocks, real estate, or other investment vehicles, strategic investing allows us to grow our assets and generate passive income streams. By conducting thorough research, diversifying our investments, and seeking professional guidance when necessary, we can navigate the complexities of the financial markets with confidence and expertise.

Despite our best efforts, financial challenges and obstacles are inevitable on the path to abundance. From debt and limited income to unexpected expenses and economic downturns, navigating these challenges requires resilience, determination, and resourcefulness. By adopting a proactive mindset, seeking alternative solutions, and focusing on solutions rather than setbacks, we can overcome financial obstacles and emerge stronger and more resilient than ever before.

Self-discipline and persistence are essential qualities for achieving long-term financial abundance and success. By cultivating self-discipline, we develop the habits and routines necessary to manage our finances effectively, resist impulse spending, and stay focused on our goals. Likewise, persistence enables us to weather the storms of uncertainty and persevere in the face of adversity, ultimately leading us towards our vision of financial freedom and prosperity.

As we conclude our exploration of practical strategies for financial manifestation, we are reminded of the transformative power that lies within each of us—the power to create our own reality, shape our financial destiny, and manifest abundance in all its forms. By incorporating these practical tips and strategies into our daily lives, we empower ourselves to transcend limitations, overcome challenges, and unlock the boundless potential for wealth and success that resides within us. May this article serve as a guiding light on your journey towards financial empowerment, fulfillment, and abundance.

The Law of Exchange: Cultivating Abundance Through Giving and Receiving

In life, the universal principle of exchange reigns supreme—a dynamic force that governs the flow of abundance and prosperity in our lives. At its essence lies the profound interplay between giving and receiving—a timeless dance of reciprocity that shapes our financial destinies and empowers us to manifest abundance in all its forms. In this article, we embark on a journey of exploration and discovery, delving into the depths of the Law of Exchange and uncovering the secrets to cultivating a mindset of abundance and trust in the universal flow of prosperity.

At the heart of the Law of Exchange lies the concept of reciprocity—the idea that what we give comes back to us in equal measure. In the realm of financial abundance, this principle manifests as a dynamic interchange of energy, wherein acts of generosity and giving create a ripple effect of abundance that flows back to us in unexpected and miraculous ways. By understanding and embracing the principle of reciprocity, we unlock the key to attracting wealth and prosperity into our lives.

Giving and receiving are intricately intertwined in the fabric of the universe, forming a symbiotic relationship that sustains the flow of abundance. Just as we give generously of our time, resources, and talents, so too must we be open to receiving the blessings and opportunities that come our way. By cultivating a mindset of abundance and gratitude, we create a receptive channel through which abundance can flow freely into our lives, enriching us on both material and spiritual levels.

Acts of generosity serve as catalysts for abundance, igniting a chain reaction of positive energy and goodwill that reverberates throughout the cosmos. Whether through charitable giving, random acts of kindness, or simply offering a helping hand to those in need, each act of generosity sends a powerful signal to the universe that we are open to receiving abundance in return. By giving freely and without expectation, we create a magnetic field of abundance that attracts prosperity into our lives with effortless grace.

Central to the Law of Exchange is the cultivation of a mindset of abundance and trust—a belief in the inherent abundance of the universe and the unwavering faith that our needs will always be met. By releasing limiting beliefs of scarcity and lack, we open ourselves to the infinite possibilities that surround us, trusting in the divine intelligence that governs the cosmos. Through affirmations, visualization, and daily practices of gratitude, we reaffirm our connection to the universal flow of prosperity, aligning ourselves with the highest vibrations of abundance.

Practical Tips for Applying the Law of Exchange

> Practice Generosity: Look for opportunities to give generously of your time, resources, and talents, knowing that each act of generosity plants seeds of abundance that will bear fruit in due time.

> Be Open to Receiving: Cultivate a mindset of receptivity and openness to receiving the blessings and opportunities that come your way. Practice saying "yes" to abundance in all its forms, trusting that the universe has your back.

> Trust in Divine Timing: Release the need to control outcomes and trust in the divine timing of the universe. Know that everything happens in perfect order and that

abundance is always flowing towards you, even when it may not seem apparent.

Express Gratitude Daily: Take time each day to express gratitude for the abundance already present in your life and for the blessings yet to come. Gratitude is the gateway to abundance, opening the floodgates of prosperity and abundance in your life.

As we conclude our exploration of the Law of Exchange, we are reminded of the profound wisdom that underlies this universal principle—a wisdom that transcends time and space, guiding us towards greater levels of abundance, prosperity, and fulfillment. By understanding and applying the principles of reciprocity, giving, and receiving, we unlock the key to a life of abundance and joy, where prosperity flows freely and effortlessly into our lives. May this article serve as a beacon of inspiration and empowerment, guiding you towards financial abundance and spiritual fulfillment.

Overcoming Financial Blocks and Cultivating Prosperity Mindset

In the intricate landscape of personal finance, our beliefs and mindset play a pivotal role in shaping our financial reality. Yet, for many, deeply ingrained limiting beliefs and financial blocks hinder their journey towards abundance and prosperity. In this comprehensive guide, we embark on a journey of self-discovery and empowerment, exploring practical strategies for overcoming financial blocks and cultivating a mindset of prosperity and abundance.

At the core of our financial challenges lie a myriad of blocks and limiting beliefs that sabotage our efforts towards financial success. From the fear of failure to the scarcity mindset and beliefs of unworthiness, these inner barriers act as roadblocks, preventing us from reaching our true potential. By identifying and understanding these blocks, we can begin the process of dismantling them and creating space for abundance to flow into our lives.

One of the most common barriers to financial success is the fear of failure—the paralyzing belief that taking risks will inevitably lead to loss and disappointment. However, it is often through failure that we learn and grow the most. By reframing failure as an opportunity for growth and resilience, we can liberate ourselves from the grip of fear and embrace the inherent risks that come with pursuing our financial goals.

Another prevalent barrier to financial abundance is the scarcity mindset—the pervasive belief that there is never enough to go around. This scarcity mentality breeds feelings of anxiety, competition, and inadequacy, perpetuating a cycle of lack and limitation. To overcome this mindset, we must shift our focus from scarcity to abundance, cultivating a mindset of gratitude and abundance. Through daily practices of gratitude, visualization, and affirmations, we can rewire our brains to see abundance where once there was only lack.

Our beliefs about money are often deeply ingrained, shaped by our upbringing, culture, and past experiences. These limiting beliefs can manifest as feelings of unworthiness, guilt, or shame around money, preventing us from achieving financial success. To rewrite our money story, we must first identify and challenge these beliefs, replacing them with empowering narratives that align with our financial goals and aspirations. Through self-reflection, journaling, and working with a coach or therapist, we can uncover and transform these limiting beliefs, paving the way for a new chapter of financial abundance.

Practical Strategies for Overcoming Financial Blocks

Affirmations and Mantras: Use positive affirmations and mantras to reprogram your subconscious mind and reinforce empowering beliefs about money and abundance. Repeat these affirmations daily to instill a sense of confidence and optimism.

Visualization and Creative Visualization: Visualize your financial goals as already achieved, imagining yourself living the life of abundance you desire. Engage all your senses in the visualization process, making the experience as vivid and real as possible.

Reframing Techniques: Challenge negative thoughts and beliefs about money by reframing them in a more positive and empowering light. For example, instead of seeing setbacks as failures, view them as opportunities for growth and learning.

Gratitude Practices: Cultivate a daily practice of gratitude for the abundance already present in your life, no matter how small. By focusing on what you have rather than what you lack, you invite more blessings and abundance into your life.

As we conclude our exploration of overcoming financial blocks and cultivating a prosperity mindset, we are reminded of the profound impact our beliefs and mindset have on our financial well-being. By courageously confronting our fears, shifting from scarcity to abundance, and rewriting our money story, we open ourselves to a world of limitless possibilities and opportunities. May this guide serve as a beacon of inspiration and empowerment on your journey towards financial abundance and fulfillment.

Chapter 5: Nurturing Health and Well-being

In life, woven with myriad experiences and endeavors, there exists a profound quest that transcends material possessions and worldly achievements – the pursuit of health and well-being. Chapter 5 of our journey delves deep into the realms of Nurturing Health and Well-being, guiding us towards the radiant path of holistic wellness.

Health, both physical and mental, forms the cornerstone of our existence, laying the foundation upon which we build our aspirations, dreams, and aspirations. In this chapter, we embark on a transformative journey, exploring the intricate interplay of mind, body, and spirit, and uncovering the profound wisdom that lies at the heart of holistic wellness.

At the core of Nurturing Health and Well-being lies the profound realization that true wellness encompasses far more than the absence of illness or disease. It encompasses vitality, resilience, and a deep-seated sense of balance and harmony that permeates every facet of our being. As we navigate the complexities of modern life, it becomes imperative to cultivate practices that nourish and sustain our physical, emotional, and spiritual well-being.

Our journey begins with Manifesting Vibrant Health, where we delve into the essence of vitality and explore the transformative power of intention and conscious living. Through the lens of abundance, we unravel the secrets of attracting radiant health and vitality, harnessing the innate wisdom of the body-mind connection to foster holistic well-being.

In our exploration of Healing Techniques and Practices, we embark on a sacred odyssey through the vast tapestry of holistic healing modalities, from ancient wisdom traditions to modern integrative therapies. From the gentle touch of energy healing to the potent healing properties of herbal medicine, we discover a treasure trove of healing practices that restore balance, rejuvenate the spirit, and awaken the body's innate healing intelligence.

As we journey deeper into the realms of holistic wellness, we encounter the profound truth of Aligning Mind, Body, and Spirit.

Here, we explore the interconnectedness of our being and the pivotal role of alignment in fostering vibrant health and well-being. Through mindfulness practices, spiritual exploration, and mindful living, we cultivate a sense of inner harmony that reverberates through every aspect of our lives.

In the pursuit of Nurturing Health and Well-being, we are called to embrace a holistic approach that honors the intricate dance of mind, body, and spirit. It is a journey of self-discovery, self-care, and self-compassion – a journey that invites us to reclaim our innate wisdom and awaken to the profound interconnectedness of all life.

As we embark on this transformative odyssey, may we be guided by the light of awareness, the power of intention, and the boundless potential of the human spirit. May our exploration of Nurturing Health and Well-being be a source of inspiration, empowerment, and profound transformation, illuminating the path to radiant vitality, inner peace, and holistic wellness.

Join us as we embark on this sacred journey of self-discovery and renewal, and together, let us embrace the radiant path of holistic wellness, one step at a time. Welcome to Chapter 5: Nurturing Health and Well-being – where the journey begins anew, and the possibilities are limitless.

Cultivating Vibrant Health: A Holistic Approach to Wellness

In the pursuit of a fulfilling life, there exists a profound quest that transcends mere existence – the quest for vibrant health. Vibrant health embodies a state of well-being that extends beyond physical vitality to encompass mental clarity, emotional resilience, and spiritual harmony. It is the cornerstone upon which we build our aspirations, dreams, and endeavors, guiding us towards a life of purpose, passion, and fulfillment.

Vibrant health is more than just the absence of illness; it is a dynamic state of vitality and wellness that permeates every aspect of our being. It encompasses physical fitness, mental clarity, emotional balance, and spiritual alignment, creating a harmonious synergy that nourishes the body, mind, and spirit. Vibrant health empowers us to live life to the fullest, unleashing our full potential and enabling us to thrive in all areas of our lives.

At the heart of manifesting vibrant health lies the power of intention – the conscious choice to cultivate optimal well-being in all aspects of our lives. By setting clear intentions for vibrant health, we harness the innate power of the mind-body connection to create a profound shift in our overall well-being. Intention acts as a guiding force, directing our thoughts, actions, and behaviors towards habits and practices that support vibrant health and vitality.

Cultivating vibrant health begins with nurturing our bodies and minds through healthy lifestyle practices. Regular exercise, adequate sleep, hydration, and stress management form the cornerstone of a vibrant lifestyle, nourishing our physical, mental, and emotional well-being. By prioritizing balance and moderation in diet and daily routines, we create a solid foundation for vibrant health to flourish.

Incorporating mindful movement practices into our daily lives is a powerful way to enhance our physical fitness and well-being. Practices such as yoga, tai chi, or qigong not only promote strength, flexibility, and balance but also cultivate inner harmony and peace. By mindfully engaging in movement and exercise, we deepen our connection to our bodies and cultivate a profound sense of presence and awareness.

Nutrition plays a pivotal role in supporting vibrant health and vitality. A balanced and nutrient-rich diet is essential for nourishing our bodies and providing the fuel needed for optimal functioning. Emphasizing whole foods, plant-based nutrition, and mindful eating habits ensures that we receive the essential nutrients our bodies need to thrive. By prioritizing nutrition and wellness, we lay the groundwork for vibrant health to flourish and thrive.

Cultivating vibrant health is a holistic journey that encompasses physical, mental, emotional, and spiritual well-being. By embracing the power of intention, adopting healthy lifestyle practices, incorporating mindful movement and exercise, and prioritizing nutrition and wellness, we empower ourselves to manifest vibrant health and vitality in our lives. May this journey be a source of inspiration, empowerment, and profound transformation, guiding us towards a life of vibrant health, happiness, and fulfillment.

Exploring Healing Modalities: A Comprehensive Guide to Holistic Wellness

In holistic wellness, healing modalities stand as vibrant threads, weaving together the physical, emotional, and energetic aspects of our being. From ancient practices rooted in tradition to modern techniques grounded in science, these modalities offer diverse pathways to healing and transformation. In this comprehensive guide, we embark on a journey to explore the rich tapestry of healing techniques and practices that nourish the body, mind, and spirit.

Healing modalities encompass a diverse array of holistic approaches to health and wellness, each offering unique insights and techniques for restoring balance and promoting healing. From acupuncture and herbal medicine to energy healing and bodywork therapies, these modalities draw upon ancient wisdom and modern science to address the root causes of illness and imbalance. By recognizing the interconnectedness of mind, body, and spirit, these modalities offer a holistic framework for promoting health and well-being on all levels.

At the heart of many healing modalities lies the principle of energy healing, which acknowledges the presence of subtle energy fields that permeate the body and influence our health and vitality. Reiki, a Japanese healing technique, is one such modality that harnesses the body's natural healing energies to promote relaxation, reduce stress, and support overall well-being. By channeling universal life force energy through gentle touch or non-touch techniques, Reiki practitioners facilitate the flow of energy to areas of imbalance, promoting healing and restoring harmony to the body, mind, and spirit.

Mind-body therapies offer powerful tools for promoting healing and wellness by addressing the intimate connection between our thoughts, emotions, and physical health. Practices such as meditation, mindfulness, and guided imagery enable us to cultivate present-moment awareness, reduce stress, and enhance emotional resilience. By quieting the mind and tuning into the wisdom of the body, these practices empower us to tap into our innate healing potential and cultivate a profound sense of well-being.

Herbal remedies and natural medicine offer a time-honored approach to health and healing, drawing upon the medicinal properties of plants to support the body's innate healing processes. From botanical supplements and herbal teas to tinctures and extracts, plant-based remedies provide a wealth of therapeutic benefits for a wide range of health concerns. By embracing the wisdom of nature and incorporating these remedies into our daily lives, we can nourish our bodies, promote healing, and enhance our overall vitality and well-being.

Central to the healing journey is the practice of self-care, which invites us to prioritize our physical, emotional, and spiritual well-being on a daily basis. Self-care practices such as relaxation techniques, self-reflection, and creative expression offer essential tools for nurturing ourselves and restoring balance in our lives. By carving out time for self-care and honoring our own needs, we cultivate resilience, strengthen our connection to ourselves, and deepen our capacity for healing and transformation.

Healing modalities offer a holistic framework for promoting health and well-being on all levels of our being. From energy healing and mind-body therapies to herbal remedies and self-care practices, these modalities empower us to tap into our innate healing potential and embrace a life of vitality, resilience, and balance. May this exploration of healing modalities inspire and empower you on your own journey to wellness, guiding you towards a state of profound healing, wholeness, and well-being.

Achieving Holistic Wellness: Aligning Mind, Body, and Spirit for Vitality and Balance

In the bustling rhythm of modern life, the pursuit of wellness extends beyond physical health to encompass a holistic approach that integrates mind, body, and spirit. This interconnectedness forms the foundation of holistic wellness, a dynamic state of being that nurtures a sense of wholeness, vitality, and balance. In this comprehensive exploration, we delve into the profound relationship between mind, body, and spirit, and discover practical strategies for aligning these aspects to foster greater well-being and inner harmony.

At the heart of holistic wellness lies the recognition that true health encompasses more than just the absence of disease—it encompasses a state of balance and integration on all levels of being. By aligning mind, body, and spirit, individuals can cultivate a profound sense of wholeness that nourishes their overall well-being and vitality. This holistic approach acknowledges the interconnectedness of all aspects of the self and emphasizes the importance of addressing underlying imbalances to promote lasting health and wellness.

The intricate relationship between the mind and body forms the cornerstone of holistic wellness, influencing everything from our physical health to our emotional well-being. Thoughts, emotions, and beliefs can profoundly impact our physiological processes, shaping our health outcomes and overall quality of life. Stress, trauma, and unresolved emotions can disrupt this connection, leading to a cascade of negative effects on both mental and physical health. By cultivating awareness of this mind-body connection, individuals can harness the power of their thoughts and emotions to promote healing, resilience, and vitality.

Spirituality plays a vital role in fostering well-being and inner harmony, offering a pathway for individuals to connect with the deeper aspects of themselves and the world around them. Spiritual practices such as meditation, prayer, and mindfulness provide valuable tools for cultivating presence, inner peace, and a sense of purpose and meaning in life. By nurturing our spiritual selves, we can tap into a source of strength and resilience that transcends the challenges of everyday life, guiding us towards greater fulfillment and wholeness.

Incorporating mindfulness into daily life is essential for aligning mind, body, and spirit and fostering holistic wellness. Mindfulness practices encourage individuals to cultivate present-moment awareness, allowing them to observe their thoughts, emotions, and sensations without judgment. By cultivating this quality of presence, individuals can develop greater self-awareness, emotional balance, and resilience in the face of life's challenges. Practical tips for incorporating mindfulness into daily life include mindfulness meditation, mindful eating, and mindful movement practices such as yoga or tai chi.

Holistic healing systems such as Traditional Chinese Medicine (TCM), Ayurveda, and Indigenous healing traditions offer valuable insights into the interconnectedness of mind, body, and spirit in the healing process. These systems view health and wellness from a holistic perspective, considering the individual as a complex interplay of physical, emotional, and spiritual energies. By addressing imbalances on multiple levels, these healing modalities offer comprehensive approaches to promoting health and vitality that honor the innate wisdom of the body and spirit.

Achieving holistic wellness requires a commitment to aligning mind, body, and spirit in harmony. By recognizing the profound interconnectedness of these aspects of self and nurturing them through mindfulness, spiritual practices, and holistic healing modalities, individuals can cultivate a profound sense of wholeness, vitality, and balance that permeates every aspect of their lives. May this exploration of holistic wellness inspire and empower you on your own journey towards greater well-being and inner harmony.

Nourishing Wellness: The Power of Holistic Nutrition for Vibrant Health

In the pursuit of optimal health and vitality, the importance of holistic nutrition cannot be overstated. Holistic nutrition goes beyond mere calorie counting or macronutrient ratios; it embraces a comprehensive approach to nourishing the body, mind, and spirit. In this enlightening exploration, we delve into the principles of holistic nutrition and discover how mindful food choices can support overall well-being and vitality.

At the core of holistic nutrition lies the belief that food is more than just fuel—it is medicine for the body and nourishment for the soul. Holistic nutrition emphasizes the consumption of whole, nutrient-dense foods that provide the body with essential vitamins, minerals, antioxidants, and phytonutrients. By focusing on the quality of food rather than just its caloric content, individuals can support optimal health, enhance vitality, and prevent disease.

Whole foods form the foundation of a holistic nutrition approach, providing the body with essential nutrients in their most natural and bioavailable forms. Fruits, vegetables, whole grains, legumes, nuts, seeds, and lean proteins are all examples of nutrient-dense whole foods that support overall health and well-being. By prioritizing whole foods in their diet, individuals can optimize nutrient intake, support digestive health, and promote a balanced microbiome.

Balanced meals are key to sustaining energy levels, supporting metabolic function, and maintaining overall well-being. A balanced meal typically consists of a variety of macronutrients, including carbohydrates, proteins, and healthy fats, along with plenty of colorful fruits and vegetables. By incorporating a diverse array of nutrient-rich foods into each meal, individuals can ensure they are meeting their nutritional needs and supporting optimal health.

Superfoods are nutrient-packed foods that are particularly rich in vitamins, minerals, and antioxidants. Examples of superfoods include berries, leafy greens, nuts, seeds, fatty fish, and fermented foods like yogurt and kimchi. These nutrient powerhouses offer a wide range of health benefits, from supporting immune function and reducing inflammation to promoting heart health and cognitive function. By incorporating superfoods into their diet, individuals can boost their nutrient intake and enhance overall well-being.

Mindful eating is a practice that involves paying attention to the sensory experience of eating and cultivating a non-judgmental awareness of food choices, hunger cues, and eating habits. By slowing down and savoring each bite, individuals can foster a deeper connection with their food and their body's nutritional needs. Mindful eating can help prevent overeating, promote healthier food choices, and enhance digestion and nutrient absorption.

Practical Tips for Holistic Nutrition

Incorporating holistic nutrition into daily life is easier than you might think. Here are some practical tips for embracing a holistic approach to nutrition and wellness:

> Prioritize whole, nutrient-dense foods in your diet, such as fruits, vegetables, whole grains, lean proteins, and healthy fats.

> Aim to fill your plate with a variety of colors, flavors, and textures to ensure a diverse range of nutrients.

Choose organic and locally sourced foods whenever possible to minimize exposure to pesticides and support environmental sustainability.

Drink plenty of water throughout the day to stay hydrated and support cellular function.

Practice mindful eating by chewing slowly, savoring each bite, and paying attention to hunger and fullness cues.

Experiment with incorporating superfoods into your meals and snacks to boost nutritional content and support overall well-being.

Listen to your body and honor its unique nutritional needs, making adjustments as necessary to support optimal health and vitality.

By embracing the principles of holistic nutrition and making mindful food choices, individuals can nourish their bodies, support their health, and enhance their overall well-being. May this exploration of holistic nutrition inspire you to cultivate a deeper connection with your food and embrace the transformative power of nourishment from within.

Finding Calm Within Chaos: The Power of Stress Management and Mindfulness

In today's fast-paced world, stress has become an inevitable part of daily life for many individuals. From demanding work schedules to personal responsibilities and unforeseen challenges, the pressures of modern living can take a toll on our mental and emotional well-being. However, amidst the chaos, there lies a powerful antidote: mindfulness. In this enlightening exploration, we delve into effective stress management techniques and the transformative role of mindfulness in promoting mental and emotional resilience.

Before we explore stress management strategies, it's essential to understand the physiological effects of stress on the body and mind. When faced with perceived threats or challenges, the body's stress response, also known as the fight-or-flight response, is triggered. This response initiates a cascade of physiological changes, including the release of stress hormones such as cortisol and adrenaline, increased heart rate, and heightened alertness. While this response is adaptive in the short term, chronic stress can have detrimental effects on both physical and mental health, contributing to a range of conditions such as anxiety, depression, insomnia, and cardiovascular disease.

Mindfulness offers a powerful antidote to the negative effects of stress, providing individuals with the tools to cultivate greater awareness, presence, and resilience in the face of life's challenges. At its core, mindfulness involves paying attention to the present moment with openness, curiosity, and acceptance. By practicing mindfulness, individuals can learn to observe their thoughts, emotions, and sensations without judgment, allowing them to respond to stressors with greater clarity and calmness.

There are many effective strategies for managing stress and promoting mental and emotional well-being through mindfulness. Here are some practical tips to incorporate mindfulness into your daily life:

> Mindful Breathing: One of the simplest and most powerful mindfulness practices is mindful breathing. Take a few moments each day to focus on your breath, noticing the sensations of inhaling and exhaling. This can help anchor your awareness in the present moment and promote relaxation.

> Body Scan Meditation: Body scan meditation involves systematically bringing awareness to different parts of the body, starting from the toes and gradually moving up to the head. This practice can help release tension and promote relaxation throughout the body.

> Mindful Movement: Engage in activities such as yoga, tai chi, or qigong, which combine movement with mindfulness and breath awareness. These practices can help reduce stress, improve flexibility, and promote overall well-being.

> Relaxation Techniques: Explore relaxation techniques such as progressive muscle relaxation, guided imagery, or visualization exercises. These practices can help calm the mind, reduce muscle tension, and induce a state of deep relaxation.

Gratitude Practice: Cultivate a daily gratitude practice by taking a few moments each day to reflect on the things you are grateful for. This can help shift your focus from stressors to blessings, fostering a more positive outlook on life.

Self-Compassion: Practice self-compassion by treating yourself with kindness, understanding, and acceptance, especially during times of stress or difficulty. Offer yourself the same compassion you would offer to a dear friend facing similar challenges.

Resilience Building: Cultivate resilience by reframing challenges as opportunities for growth and learning. Adopt a growth mindset, embrace change, and practice adaptive coping strategies to navigate life's ups and downs with greater ease.

Incorporating these mindfulness-based practices into your daily life can cultivate greater resilience, reduce stress levels, and promote overall mental and emotional well-being. May this journey of self-discovery and mindfulness lead you to a place of inner peace, balance, and harmony amidst life's inevitable challenges.

Chapter 6: Enhancing Relationships and Connection

In human existence, relationships serve as the vibrant threads that weave together the fabric of our lives. From the tender embrace of a loved one to the camaraderie shared among friends, our connections with others enrich our experiences, shape our perspectives, and define our sense of belonging in the world. As we embark on the journey of enhancing relationships and fostering deeper connections, Chapter 6 of our exploration delves into the profound realm of human interaction.

In this chapter, we embark on a voyage of self-discovery and interpersonal exploration, delving into the intricacies of manifesting fulfilling relationships, cultivating love and harmony, and strengthening social connections. As we navigate the diverse landscapes of human connection, we uncover the transformative power of intention, compassion, and authenticity in nurturing bonds that resonate with our souls.

At the heart of our exploration lies the pursuit of fulfilling relationships—connections that ignite our spirits, inspire our growth, and mirror the depths of our being. We delve into the art of manifestation, harnessing the principles of the Law of Attraction to align our intentions with the vibrant tapestry of relationships we wish to cultivate. Through self-reflection, intention setting, and mindful action, we invite into our lives the companionship, support, and love that align with our deepest desires.

Moving beyond the realm of individual connections, we immerse ourselves in the transformative journey of cultivating love and harmony within our relationships. From romantic partnerships to familial bonds and friendships, we explore the nuances of compassion, empathy, and forgiveness that form the bedrock of meaningful connections. Through open communication, mutual understanding, and acts of kindness, we nourish the seeds of love and sow the fertile grounds for harmony to flourish.

As we traverse the landscapes of human connection, we recognize the profound impact of social bonds on our well-being and sense of belonging. We embark on a quest to strengthen our social connections, weaving a rich tapestry of community, camaraderie, and support. From fostering new friendships to deepening existing ties, we embrace vulnerability, authenticity, and reciprocity as the cornerstones of meaningful social interactions.

Unveiling the Art of Manifesting Fulfilling Relationships

In the intricate dance of human connection, our relationships serve as mirrors reflecting the depths of our souls, the essence of our desires, and the landscapes of our dreams. Guided by the principles of the Law of Attraction, our thoughts, beliefs, and intentions shape the tapestry of relationships we weave, drawing into our lives those who resonate with our innermost truths. In this exploration of manifesting fulfilling relationships, we embark on a journey of self-discovery, intention setting, and inspired action to cultivate bonds that enrich our lives and nourish our souls.

At the heart of manifesting fulfilling relationships lies the profound wisdom of the Law of Attraction—a universal principle that states like attracts like. In the realm of relationships, our thoughts, beliefs, and vibrations act as magnetic forces, drawing into our lives individuals who resonate with our energy and intentions. By aligning our thoughts and beliefs with the qualities and dynamics we seek in relationships, we create a vibrational match that attracts kindred spirits into our orbit.

Central to the manifestation of fulfilling relationships is the clarity of our personal values, preferences, and intentions. By gaining insight into our authentic selves and articulating our desires with clarity and conviction, we set the stage for attracting relationships that align with our highest good. Whether seeking companionship, support, or shared passions, it is essential to discern what truly matters to us and to honor our intrinsic values in our quest for meaningful connections.

A cornerstone of manifesting fulfilling relationships is the practice of self-love and self-awareness. By nurturing a deep sense of love and acceptance for ourselves, we cultivate a magnetic energy that draws loving and supportive partners into our lives. Through self-awareness, we gain insight into our patterns, beliefs, and emotional wounds, allowing us to heal past traumas and transcend limiting beliefs that may sabotage our relationships. By tending to our inner landscape with compassion and care, we create a fertile ground for nurturing fulfilling connections with others.

Intention setting and visualization serve as powerful tools in the manifestation of fulfilling relationships. By setting clear intentions that articulate the qualities, dynamics, and experiences we seek in relationships, we align our energy with the vibrational frequency of our desires. Through visualization practices, we vividly imagine ourselves experiencing the joy, love, and fulfillment of the relationships we wish to manifest, thereby imprinting our desires onto the fabric of the universe and calling them into being.

Manifesting fulfilling relationships requires more than just intention—it calls for inspired action rooted in courage, openness, and authenticity. By stepping out of our comfort zones, engaging in new experiences, and actively seeking opportunities to connect with others, we expand our social circles and invite serendipitous encounters into our lives. Whether attending social events, joining interest-based groups, or simply striking up conversations with strangers, every interaction serves as a potential gateway to meaningful connection.

The art of manifesting fulfilling relationships encompasses a multifaceted journey of self-discovery, intention setting, and inspired action. By understanding the principles of the Law of Attraction, clarifying our values and intentions, practicing self-love and self-awareness, setting clear intentions, and taking inspired action, we pave the way for the emergence of relationships that resonate with our deepest truths and aspirations. As we embark on this transformative journey, may we open our hearts to the infinite possibilities that await us, embracing the beauty and magic of authentic connection in all its forms.

Cultivating Love and Harmony

In the intricate of human relationships, love and harmony serve as the threads that bind hearts together, weaving a fabric of connection, understanding, and mutual respect. As we navigate the ebbs and flows of our interpersonal dynamics, it is essential to cultivate love, compassion, and empathy as the guiding principles that nurture harmonious relationships. In this exploration of cultivating love and harmony, we delve into the transformative power of forgiveness, communication, kindness, and mindfulness in fostering deeper connections and fostering a sense of unity within our relationships.

At the heart of cultivating love and harmony lies the profound practice of love, compassion, and empathy. Love, as the universal force that unites souls, serves as the foundation upon which harmonious relationships are built. Compassion, the tender embrace of understanding and kindness, nurtures empathy and fosters deeper connections with others. Empathy, the ability to walk in another's shoes and resonate with their experiences, bridges the gap between hearts and fosters a sense of shared humanity. By embracing love, compassion, and empathy, we create an environment of warmth, acceptance, and understanding that nourishes the bonds of connection within our relationships.

Forgiveness, acceptance, and understanding are essential ingredients in the alchemy of cultivating love and harmony within relationships. Forgiveness, the act of releasing resentment and letting go of past hurts, liberates the heart from the shackles of pain and opens the door to healing and reconciliation. Acceptance, the gentle embrace of what is, honors the uniqueness of each individual and fosters a culture of unconditional love and respect. Understanding, the art of listening deeply and empathetically, cultivates empathy and fosters deeper connections by validating the experiences and emotions of others. By practicing forgiveness, acceptance, and understanding, we create a space of safety, trust, and vulnerability where love can flourish and harmony can prevail.

Open and honest communication serves as the cornerstone of harmonious relationships, providing a channel for expressing needs, emotions, and desires with clarity and authenticity. By fostering an environment of open dialogue and active listening, we create opportunities for mutual understanding, empathy, and connection. Honest communication invites transparency, vulnerability, and trust, laying the groundwork for resolving conflicts peacefully and strengthening the bonds of love and harmony. Whether through heartfelt conversations, compassionate listening, or nonverbal gestures of affection, open communication nurtures deeper connections and fosters a culture of emotional intimacy and mutual respect within relationships.

Acts of kindness, appreciation, and gratitude serve as potent catalysts for cultivating love and harmony within relationships. Kindness, the simple yet profound gesture of goodwill and compassion, fosters feelings of warmth, generosity, and connection. Appreciation, the heartfelt expression of gratitude and recognition, acknowledges the value and contributions of others, strengthening bonds and fostering a sense of mutual appreciation and respect. Gratitude, the practice of acknowledging and savoring the blessings in our lives, cultivates a spirit of abundance, contentment, and joy, deepening our connections and nurturing a culture of love and harmony. By engaging in acts of kindness, appreciation, and gratitude, we infuse our relationships with warmth, positivity, and love, creating a ripple effect of goodwill and connection that reverberates throughout our lives.

Mindfulness and presence serve as gateways to deeper connection, intimacy, and joy within relationships. Mindfulness, the practice of being fully present and aware in the present moment, invites us to savor the richness of each interaction, fostering deeper connections and intimacy. Presence, the art of showing up authentically and wholeheartedly in our relationships, cultivates trust, vulnerability, and authenticity, creating opportunities for deeper connection and understanding. By cultivating mindfulness and presence in our interactions, we create space for love, harmony, and joy to flourish, enriching our relationships and nourishing our souls.

The journey of cultivating love and harmony within relationships is a sacred dance of the heart, guided by the principles of love, compassion, and empathy. By practicing forgiveness, acceptance, and understanding, communicating openly and honestly, engaging in acts of kindness, appreciation, and gratitude, and cultivating mindfulness and presence, we create an environment of warmth, connection, and love that nourishes our relationships and uplifts our spirits. As we embrace these practices with an open heart and a willingness to grow, may we deepen our connections, foster harmony, and experience the profound beauty and joy of love in all its forms.

Strengthening Social Connections for Enhanced Well-being

In the tapestry of human existence, social connections serve as the colorful threads that weave together the fabric of our lives, enriching our experiences and nurturing our souls. From casual acquaintances to close friendships, the bonds we forge with others play a pivotal role in shaping our mental, emotional, and physical well-being. In this exploration of strengthening social connections, we delve into the profound impact of human connection on our lives and discover practical strategies for cultivating meaningful relationships and fostering a sense of belonging and community.

At the heart of our human experience lies the innate desire for connection and belonging. Social connections not only provide us with a sense of support and belonging but also have profound implications for our mental, emotional, and physical health. Research has shown that individuals with strong social ties experience lower rates of depression, anxiety, and stress, as well as better immune function and overall well-being. By recognizing the value of social connections, we acknowledge their power to uplift our spirits, enhance our resilience, and enrich our lives in countless ways.

Strengthening social ties involves actively engaging with others and nurturing relationships that bring joy, support, and fulfillment to our lives. One effective way to strengthen social connections is by joining social groups or clubs that align with our interests and passions. Whether it's a book club, hiking group, or volunteer organization, participating in shared activities allows us to meet like-minded individuals and forge new friendships based on common interests.

Volunteering is another powerful way to strengthen social ties while making a positive impact in our communities. By giving back to others and contributing our time and talents to worthy causes, we not only connect with fellow volunteers but also experience the intrinsic rewards of altruism and service.

Participating in community events and gatherings is yet another avenue for strengthening social connections. Whether it's a neighborhood block party, cultural festival, or charity fundraiser, community events provide opportunities to meet new people, build relationships, and foster a sense of belonging and camaraderie within our local communities.

In addition to forging new connections, it's equally important to nurture and cultivate existing friendships and relationships. Regular communication, whether through phone calls, text messages, or face-to-face interactions, is key to maintaining strong social ties and fostering a sense of closeness and intimacy.

Shared activities and experiences also play a vital role in nurturing relationships and creating meaningful connections. Whether it's going for a walk in the park, sharing a meal together, or engaging in a favorite hobby, spending quality time with loved ones strengthens bonds and creates lasting memories.

Expressing appreciation and gratitude for the people in our lives is another powerful way to nurture relationships and strengthen social connections. Taking the time to acknowledge the contributions of others and express gratitude for their presence in our lives fosters a sense of mutual appreciation and deepens the bonds of connection.

For some individuals, socializing can be challenging due to feelings of shyness, social anxiety, or fear of rejection. However, by practicing vulnerability and authenticity in social interactions, we can overcome these barriers and forge deeper connections with others. Being open and genuine about our thoughts, feelings, and experiences allows others to see us for who we truly are and fosters genuine connections based on authenticity and trust.

In today's digital age, technology and social media offer powerful tools for connecting with others and fostering social ties. However, it's important to use these platforms mindfully and intentionally, ensuring that they enhance rather than detract from our social connections.

Setting boundaries around our use of technology and social media is essential for maintaining balance and preserving the quality of our relationships. By establishing limits on screen time, practicing digital detoxes, and prioritizing face-to-face interactions, we can ensure that technology serves as a tool for enhancing our social connections rather than replacing them.

Strengthening social connections is essential for enhancing our well-being and enriching our lives. By recognizing the value of human connection, exploring different ways to strengthen social ties, nurturing existing relationships, overcoming social barriers, and utilizing technology mindfully, we can cultivate meaningful connections that bring joy, support, and fulfillment to our lives. As we continue on our journey of building bridges and fostering connections with others, may we embrace the power of human connection to uplift our spirits, deepen our relationships, and create a world filled with love, compassion, and belonging.

Key Strategies for Building Healthy Relationships

In the intricate dance of human interaction, effective communication serves as the cornerstone of healthy relationships. Whether it's with our partners, family members, friends, or colleagues, the ability to express ourselves clearly and listen empathetically fosters understanding, empathy, and mutual respect. In this article, we delve into the importance of effective communication skills and explore practical strategies for mastering the art of communication in all areas of our lives.

Effective communication is essential for building and maintaining healthy relationships. It allows us to express our thoughts, feelings, and needs clearly and assertively, while also listening attentively to others' perspectives and understanding their experiences. When communication breaks down, misunderstandings can arise, conflicts may escalate, and relationships may suffer. By honing our communication skills, we can navigate difficult conversations with grace, resolve conflicts peacefully, and strengthen the bonds of connection with those around us.

Active listening is a fundamental component of effective communication. It involves fully engaging with the speaker, paying attention to both verbal and nonverbal cues, and demonstrating empathy and understanding. To practice active listening, start by giving the speaker your full attention, maintaining eye contact, and using nonverbal gestures such as nodding and mirroring to show that you are engaged and receptive. Avoid interrupting or rushing to offer solutions, and instead focus on listening with an open mind and seeking to understand the speaker's perspective. Reflecting back what you've heard and asking clarifying questions can also demonstrate that you are truly listening and interested in the speaker's experience.

Assertive communication is another crucial aspect of effective communication. It involves expressing our thoughts, feelings, and needs in a clear, direct, and respectful manner, while also respecting the rights and boundaries of others. To practice assertive communication, start by using "I" statements to express your thoughts and feelings, rather than placing blame or making accusations. Be specific about what you want or need, and be willing to negotiate and find solutions that work for both parties. Maintain a calm and composed demeanor, even in challenging situations, and avoid resorting to passive or aggressive communication styles. By communicating assertively, you can establish healthy boundaries, build trust, and cultivate mutually satisfying relationships.

Conflict is a natural part of any relationship, but how we handle conflict can make all the difference in maintaining healthy relationships. Effective conflict resolution involves addressing disagreements constructively, seeking common ground, and finding mutually beneficial solutions. To resolve conflicts effectively, start by approaching the situation with an open mind and a willingness to listen to the other person's perspective. Focus on the underlying issues rather than getting caught up in blame or defensiveness, and strive to find win-win solutions that address the needs and concerns of both parties. Practice active listening, empathy, and assertive communication techniques to foster understanding and reach resolution collaboratively. Remember that conflicts can be opportunities for growth and learning, and by approaching them with patience, compassion, and respect, we can strengthen our relationships and deepen our connections with others.

Effective communication is the cornerstone of healthy relationships. By practicing active listening, assertive communication, and conflict resolution strategies, we can foster understanding, empathy, and mutual respect in our interactions with others. As we continue to hone our communication skills and cultivate meaningful connections, may we build stronger relationships, navigate challenges with grace, and create a world filled with empathy, understanding, and love.

The Importance of Boundaries and Self-Care

In the intricate tapestry of human connections, setting boundaries and prioritizing self-care are essential threads that weave together healthy dynamics, respect for individual needs, and overall relationship satisfaction. In this article, we delve into the significance of establishing boundaries in relationships and embracing self-care practices to maintain balance and well-being.

Boundaries are the invisible lines that define the limits and expectations within a relationship. They serve as guidelines for how we allow others to treat us, what behavior is acceptable, and what is not. Healthy boundaries foster mutual respect, trust, and understanding, while also providing a sense of safety and security within the relationship. Without clear boundaries, relationships can become fraught with misunderstandings, resentment, and conflict.

Setting boundaries is crucial for preserving our physical, emotional, and mental well-being. It allows us to protect ourselves from being taken advantage of, manipulated, or mistreated by others. By clearly communicating our needs, preferences, and limits, we empower ourselves to make informed decisions about how we engage with others and what behavior we will tolerate. Boundaries also create a framework for healthy communication, conflict resolution, and intimacy within relationships.

Practical Tips for Setting Boundaries

Identify Your Needs: Take the time to reflect on your values, priorities, and personal boundaries. What behaviors or situations make you feel uncomfortable or disrespected? What are your non-negotiables in relationships?

Communicate Clearly: When setting boundaries, be direct, assertive, and respectful. Use "I" statements to express your needs and feelings, and be specific about what you expect from others.

Enforce Consequences: Establish consequences for boundary violations and follow through with them consistently. This may involve temporarily withdrawing from the relationship, setting limits on certain behaviors, or seeking outside support if necessary.

Practice Self-Compassion: Remember that setting boundaries is an act of self-care, not selfishness. It's okay to prioritize your well-being and advocate for your needs, even if it may disappoint or upset others.

Self-care is the deliberate act of nurturing our physical, emotional, and mental health. It involves recognizing our own needs and taking proactive steps to meet them, whether it's through relaxation, hobbies, exercise, or seeking support from others. Self-care is not selfish; it's essential for maintaining balance, resilience, and overall well-being.

Prioritizing self-care is vital for maintaining a healthy relationship with ourselves and others. When we neglect our own needs, we risk becoming depleted, resentful, and emotionally unavailable to those around us. By investing time and energy into self-care practices, we replenish our reserves, boost our mood, and increase our capacity to show up fully in our relationships.

Practical Self-Care Tips

Establish Routine: Create a daily self-care routine that includes activities that nourish your mind, body, and spirit. This could include exercise, meditation, journaling, or spending time in nature.

Set Boundaries: Just as we set boundaries with others, it's essential to establish boundaries around our time, energy, and resources. Learn to say no to activities or commitments that drain you or detract from your well-being.

Practice Mindfulness: Cultivate present-moment awareness and mindfulness in your daily life. Pay attention to your thoughts, feelings, and bodily sensations without judgment, and practice self-compassion and acceptance.

Seek Support: Don't be afraid to reach out for support when you need it. Whether it's from friends, family, or a therapist, having a support system in place can provide validation, guidance, and encouragement on your self-care journey.

Setting boundaries and prioritizing self-care are essential components of building and maintaining healthy relationships. By establishing clear boundaries, we create a framework for mutual respect, understanding, and trust within our relationships. Likewise, by embracing self-care practices, we replenish our energy, cultivate resilience, and enhance our overall well-being, allowing us to show up fully in our relationships and lead fulfilling lives.

Chapter 7: Manifesting Success and Achievement

In the grand tapestry of life, success and achievement are the threads that weave together our dreams and aspirations. They are the milestones that mark our journey of growth and fulfillment, guiding us towards our highest potential. Chapter 7 of our journey delves into the realm of Manifesting Success and Achievement, where we explore the power of intention, resilience, and celebration in sculpting the life we desire.

At its core, this chapter is a testament to the human spirit's capacity to overcome obstacles, set audacious goals, and triumph against all odds. It is a roadmap for those who dare to dream big, for those who refuse to settle for mediocrity, and for those who are ready to manifest their deepest desires into reality.

The journey begins with Setting Goals and Intentions for Success, where we learn to harness the power of intentionality in shaping our destiny. Here, we delve into the art of goal-setting, exploring the importance of clarity, specificity, and purpose in defining our aspirations. Through visualization, affirmation, and strategic planning, we pave the path towards our desired outcomes, aligning our thoughts and actions with our deepest desires.

But the road to success is not without its challenges. In the face of adversity, we must summon the strength to Overcome Obstacles and Challenges, transforming setbacks into stepping stones towards greatness. Here, we learn to confront our fears, silence our inner critic, and embrace failure as a necessary stepping stone on the path to mastery. With resilience as our guiding light, we navigate the twists and turns of life with unwavering determination and unwavering faith in our ability to succeed.

Yet, amidst the trials and tribulations, it is essential to pause and celebrate our victories. In Celebrating Achievements and Milestones, we honor our progress, acknowledge our growth, and bask in the glory of our accomplishments. Here, we learn to savor the journey, reveling in each triumph, no matter how small. Through reflection, gratitude, and self-appreciation, we cultivate a sense of abundance and fulfillment that propels us towards even greater heights of success.

As we embark on this chapter of our journey, let us remember that success is not merely a destination but a way of being. It is the relentless pursuit of excellence, the unwavering commitment to our dreams, and the courage to step into our fullest potential. With intentionality, resilience, and celebration as our allies, we embark on a journey of self-discovery and transformation, manifesting success and achievement in all areas of our lives.

So, dear reader, I invite you to join me on this extraordinary adventure as we unlock the doors to our wildest dreams and manifest the life we were always meant to live. Together, let us dare to dream, dare to overcome, and dare to celebrate the boundless possibilities that await us on the path to success and achievement.

The Art of Setting Goals and Intentions

In the pursuit of success and achievement, setting goals and intentions serves as the compass that guides us towards our desired destination. Whether it's personal growth, career advancement, or realizing our dreams, the clarity and focus provided by well-defined goals propel us forward on our journey. In this article, we explore the foundational principles of goal setting, from understanding its importance to practical techniques for effective implementation.

Goal setting is the cornerstone of success, providing a roadmap for our aspirations and dreams. By defining clear and achievable goals, we create a sense of purpose and direction in our lives. Goals serve as the blueprint for our actions, helping us prioritize tasks, stay motivated, and measure progress along the way. Without clear goals, we risk drifting aimlessly and falling short of our true potential.

Types of Goals:

Goals come in various shapes and sizes, each serving a distinct purpose in our pursuit of success. Short-term goals provide immediate focus and motivation, while long-term goals offer a vision for the future. Personal goals encompass areas such as health, relationships, and personal development, while professional goals pertain to career advancement and achievement. By identifying and aligning these different types of goals, we create a holistic framework for success in all aspects of our lives.

SMART Goals: The SMART criteria offer a practical framework for setting effective goals that are Specific, Measurable, Achievable, Relevant, and Time-bound. Specific goals provide clarity and direction by clearly defining what we want to achieve. Measurable goals enable us to track progress and evaluate success objectively. Achievable goals are realistic and within our capabilities, ensuring that we maintain motivation and momentum. Relevant goals align with our values, aspirations, and long-term vision, ensuring that our efforts are meaningful and purposeful. Time-bound goals have a clear deadline or timeframe, instilling a sense of urgency and accountability.

Visualization and Affirmation: Visualization and affirmation techniques are powerful tools for reinforcing goals and intentions and aligning the subconscious mind with desired outcomes. Visualization involves mentally picturing oneself achieving a specific goal or desired outcome, engaging all the senses to create a vivid and compelling image of success. Affirmations are positive statements or declarations that affirm our ability to achieve our goals, reinforcing belief in ourselves and our potential. By regularly practicing visualization and affirmations, we program our subconscious mind for success, overcoming limiting beliefs and cultivating a mindset of abundance and possibility.

Setting goals and intentions for success is not merely about wishful thinking; it's about taking deliberate and strategic steps towards realizing our dreams. By understanding the importance of goal setting, embracing the SMART criteria, and harnessing the power of visualization and affirmation, we empower ourselves to manifest our deepest desires and aspirations. As we embark on this journey of self-discovery and growth, let us remember that success is not a destination but a journey, and it begins with the first step of setting clear and achievable goals.

Strategies for Overcoming Obstacles and Challenges

On the path to success, obstacles and challenges are inevitable. From self-doubt to external setbacks, these roadblocks can often feel insurmountable, threatening to derail our progress and undermine our confidence. However, with the right mindset and strategies, we can navigate through adversity and emerge stronger than ever. In this article, we explore practical techniques for overcoming obstacles, embracing resilience, and turning setbacks into opportunities for growth and self-improvement.

Obstacles come in various forms, both internal and external. Internal obstacles may include fear of failure, self-doubt, limiting beliefs, and negative self-talk. External obstacles can range from financial constraints and lack of resources to unforeseen challenges and setbacks. By recognizing and understanding these obstacles, we can better prepare ourselves to tackle them head-on and navigate through adversity with resilience and determination.

Strategies for Overcoming Obstacles:

Reframing Negative Thoughts: One of the most effective ways to overcome obstacles is to reframe negative thoughts and beliefs into positive affirmations. Instead of dwelling on perceived failures or limitations, focus on strengths, opportunities, and solutions. By shifting your mindset from one of scarcity to abundance, you empower yourself to overcome challenges with confidence and creativity.

Seeking Support: Don't be afraid to reach out for help when facing obstacles. Whether it's seeking advice from mentors, sharing your struggles with trusted friends or family members, or joining support groups, having a strong support network can provide valuable guidance, encouragement, and perspective.

Developing Problem-Solving Skills: Cultivate your problem-solving skills by approaching obstacles with a proactive and solution-oriented mindset. Break down complex challenges into smaller, manageable tasks, and brainstorm potential solutions. By approaching obstacles with curiosity and creativity, you can uncover innovative solutions and overcome even the most daunting challenges.

Resilience is the ability to bounce back from setbacks, adapt to change, and thrive in the face of adversity. Cultivating resilience involves developing coping mechanisms, maintaining a positive outlook, and learning from past experiences. Embrace challenges as opportunities for growth and transformation, rather than insurmountable barriers. By building resilience, you can navigate through life's ups and downs with grace and resilience.

Failure is not the end of the road but rather a stepping stone on the path to success. Embrace failure as a valuable learning experience and an opportunity for growth and self-improvement. Reflect on past failures with curiosity and humility, identifying lessons learned and areas for improvement. By reframing failure as feedback and adjusting your approach accordingly, you can turn setbacks into stepping stones towards greater success and fulfillment.

Obstacles and challenges are an inevitable part of the journey to success, but they need not define our destiny. By understanding the nature of obstacles, adopting effective strategies for overcoming them, embracing resilience, and learning from failure, we can navigate through adversity with courage, confidence, and determination. Remember, it's not the absence of obstacles that defines success, but rather our ability to overcome them and emerge stronger on the other side.

The Art of Celebrating Achievements and Milestones

In the journey of life, accomplishments and milestones serve as markers of progress and growth. Whether big or small, each achievement is a testament to our hard work, dedication, and perseverance. Yet, all too often, we overlook the importance of celebrating these victories. In this article, we delve into the significance of celebrating achievements and milestones, reflecting on progress, rewarding success, and setting new goals to continue the cycle of growth and achievement.

Celebrating achievements and milestones is not merely about indulging in fleeting moments of joy; it is about recognizing our accomplishments, honoring our efforts, and acknowledging our worth. By celebrating our successes, we reinforce positive behavior, boost confidence, and maintain motivation to pursue our goals with renewed vigor and enthusiasm. Celebration serves as a powerful reminder of our capabilities and strengths, instilling a sense of pride and fulfillment in our accomplishments.

Amidst the hustle and bustle of daily life, it's easy to lose sight of how far we've come. Yet, taking the time to reflect on our progress is essential for maintaining perspective and cultivating gratitude. Whether through journaling, meditation, or simply quiet contemplation, carving out moments to acknowledge our achievements allows us to bask in the glow of our success and gain clarity on our path forward. No accomplishment is too small to celebrate, and each milestone reached is a cause for celebration.

Celebrating achievements is not only about acknowledging our successes but also about rewarding ourselves for our hard work and dedication. Whether it's treating ourselves to a special experience, indulging in a favorite activity, or simply taking time to relax and recharge, finding meaningful ways to reward ourselves reinforces positive behavior and reinforces the value of our achievements. Moreover, sharing our successes with loved ones allows us to deepen our connections and bask in the support and encouragement of those who matter most to us.

As we celebrate our achievements and milestones, it's essential to remember that success is not a destination but a journey. Setting new goals and intentions after achieving success allows us to continue the cycle of growth and achievement, propelling us forward towards new heights of success and fulfillment. By embracing the process of continuous improvement and setting our sights on new challenges, we keep the flame of motivation burning bright and ensure that our journey towards success remains dynamic and fulfilling.

Celebrating achievements and milestones is an essential aspect of the journey towards success and fulfillment. By taking the time to reflect on our progress, reward ourselves for our successes, and set new goals for the future, we honor our efforts, cultivate gratitude, and maintain motivation to pursue our dreams. So, let us embrace the art of celebration, revel in our achievements, and continue to strive for greatness with passion, purpose, and perseverance.

Strategies for Developing a Growth Mindset

In the pursuit of success and personal growth, our mindset plays a pivotal role. A growth mindset, characterized by a belief in one's ability to learn, adapt, and improve, serves as a powerful catalyst for achievement and resilience. In contrast to a fixed mindset, which views abilities as innate and unchangeable, a growth mindset embraces challenges as opportunities for learning and growth. In this article, we explore the concept of a growth mindset and discuss strategies for cultivating this mindset to achieve success and personal development.

Understanding the Growth Mindset:

At the heart of a growth mindset lies the belief that intelligence, talents, and abilities can be developed through dedication, effort, and perseverance. Individuals with a growth mindset view challenges, setbacks, and criticism as opportunities for learning and improvement, rather than obstacles to success. They approach tasks with a sense of curiosity, resilience, and optimism, knowing that their abilities are not fixed but can be developed over time through deliberate practice and continuous learning.

Strategies for Cultivating a Growth Mindset:

> Embrace Challenges: Rather than shying away from challenges, embrace them as opportunities for growth and learning. Challenge yourself to step outside your comfort zone, tackle new tasks, and take on projects that stretch your abilities. By facing challenges head-on and persevering in the face of adversity, you develop resilience, confidence, and a sense of mastery.

> Adopt a Learning Mindset: Cultivate a lifelong love of learning by adopting a mindset focused on growth and development. Approach every experience as an opportunity to gain new knowledge, skills, and insights. Seek out feedback from others, welcome constructive criticism, and view mistakes as valuable learning opportunities rather than failures.

> Cultivate Resilience: Develop resilience in the face of setbacks and obstacles by reframing setbacks as temporary setbacks rather than permanent failures. Practice resilience-building techniques such as positive self-talk, reframing negative thoughts, and focusing on solutions rather than dwelling on problems. Remember that setbacks are a natural part of the learning process and an opportunity to bounce back stronger than before.

> Foster a Growth-Oriented Environment: Surround yourself with individuals who embody a growth mindset and support your aspirations for growth and development. Seek out

mentors, coaches, and peers who inspire and challenge you to reach your full potential. Create a supportive environment that encourages experimentation, innovation, and continuous improvement.

Celebrate Progress: Acknowledge and celebrate your progress and achievements along the way. Take pride in your efforts, no matter how small, and recognize the strides you've made towards your goals. By celebrating your progress, you reinforce positive behavior, boost confidence, and maintain motivation to continue growing and evolving.

Cultivating a growth mindset is essential for achieving success and personal growth in all areas of life. By embracing challenges, adopting a learning mindset, cultivating resilience, fostering a growth-oriented environment, and celebrating progress, you can develop the mindset necessary to overcome obstacles, achieve your goals, and unlock your full potential. So, embrace the journey of growth, cultivate a mindset of possibility and potential, and watch as you transform challenges into opportunities and dreams into reality.

Building Resilience in the Face of Failure

Failure is an inevitable part of the journey to success, yet it can often feel like a devastating blow to our confidence and motivation. However, it is not the failure itself that defines us but rather how we respond to it. Resilience, the ability to bounce back from setbacks and adversity, plays a crucial role in navigating the ups and downs of life and ultimately achieving our goals. In this article, we delve into the importance of resilience in the face of failure and provide practical tips and techniques for building resilience and overcoming obstacles on the path to success.

Understanding Resilience:

Resilience is the capacity to adapt and thrive in the face of adversity, setbacks, and challenges. It involves maintaining a positive outlook, bouncing back from failures, and persevering in the pursuit of our goals. Resilient individuals possess the ability to learn from their experiences, develop coping strategies, and maintain a sense of optimism and determination despite obstacles.

Practical Tips for Building Resilience:

Embrace Failure as a Learning Opportunity: Instead of viewing failure as a reflection of your worth or abilities, reframe it as a valuable learning experience. Reflect on what went wrong, identify areas for improvement, and extract lessons that can help you grow and evolve. By viewing failure as feedback rather than defeat, you empower yourself to learn and grow from every setback.

Cultivate Self-Compassion: Treat yourself with kindness, understanding, and compassion in the face of failure. Acknowledge the disappointment and frustration you may feel, but avoid self-criticism and negative self-talk. Practice self-compassion by offering yourself the same level of care and support you would offer to a friend facing a similar situation.

Focus on What You Can Control: While some factors leading to failure may be beyond your control, focus on the aspects you can influence. Channel your energy into taking proactive steps to address the situation, develop new strategies, and move forward. By focusing on what you can control, you regain a sense of agency and empowerment over your circumstances.

Cultivate Optimism and Resilience Mindset: Adopting a mindset of optimism and resilience can help you navigate setbacks with greater ease and determination. Cultivate optimism by focusing on the positive aspects of your experiences, maintaining a sense of hope for the future, and reframing challenges as opportunities for growth. By cultivating a resilience mindset, you strengthen your ability to bounce back from failures and setbacks with resilience and determination.

Seek Support and Connection: Don't be afraid to reach out for support from friends, family, mentors, or support groups during challenging times. Sharing your experiences with others can provide perspective, encouragement, and emotional support. Surround yourself with a supportive network of individuals who believe in your abilities and offer encouragement and guidance when needed.

Practice Self-Care: Prioritize self-care activities that nurture your physical, emotional, and mental well-being, especially during times of stress and adversity. Engage in activities that bring you joy, relaxation, and fulfillment, such as exercise, meditation, hobbies, or spending time in nature. Taking care of yourself enables you to recharge your energy, build resilience, and face challenges with greater strength and resilience.

Building resilience in the face of failure is essential for navigating life's challenges and achieving success. By embracing failure as a learning opportunity, cultivating self-compassion, focusing on what you can control, cultivating optimism and resilience mindset, seeking support and connection, and practicing self-care, you can strengthen your resilience and bounce back from setbacks more muscular and more determined. So, embrace failure as a stepping stone to growth, resilience as your superpower, and watch as you rise solid and resilient in the face of adversity.

Chapter 8: Integrating Manifestation Practices into Daily Life

In our quest for personal growth, fulfillment, and success, we often seek tools and techniques to help us manifest our deepest desires and aspirations. Chapter 8 of our journey delves into the transformative realm of integrating manifestation practices into our daily lives. This chapter serves as a guide for harnessing the power of intention, aligning with universal abundance, and co-creating our reality through intentional action and conscious awareness.

Integrating manifestation practices into our daily routines empowers us to cultivate a mindset of abundance, clarity, and purpose. It is a journey of self-discovery and empowerment, where we learn to tap into the infinite potential that resides within us and unlock the secrets of manifesting our dreams into reality.

In this chapter we explore various manifestation rituals, techniques, and principles that can be seamlessly woven into our daily lives. From setting clear intentions to maintaining consistency and staying open to opportunities, each aspect of manifestation holds the key to unlocking our fullest potential and creating a life filled with meaning, joy, and abundance.

Creating Your Manifestation Ritual

In the pursuit of our dreams and desires, we often seek ways to align our thoughts, intentions, and actions with the outcomes we wish to manifest. One powerful method to amplify the manifestation process is by incorporating manifestation rituals into our daily lives. These rituals serve as intentional practices that help us focus our energy, clarify our intentions, and cultivate the mindset needed to attract our desired outcomes. In this article, we will delve into the significance of manifestation rituals, explore different types of rituals, provide guidance on designing a personalized ritual, and highlight the importance of consistency and commitment in this transformative process.

Manifestation rituals hold profound significance in our journey towards achieving our goals and aspirations. By engaging in these rituals, we create a sacred space for manifestation, where we can connect with our innermost desires and communicate them to the universe. These rituals serve as symbolic gestures of our commitment to our dreams, signaling to the universe our readiness to receive the blessings we seek. Moreover, manifestation rituals help us align our thoughts, emotions, and actions with our intentions, fostering a state of alignment and coherence conducive to manifestation.

There are various manifestation rituals that individuals can incorporate into their daily routines to enhance the manifestation process. One popular ritual is visualization, where individuals mentally picture themselves achieving their goals and experiencing the desired outcomes with vivid detail and emotion. Affirmations are another powerful ritual, where individuals repeat positive statements or mantras that affirm their beliefs and intentions. Scripting involves writing down one's desires and intentions as if they have already manifested, thereby programming the subconscious mind for success.

Gratitude journaling is a manifestation ritual that involves regularly writing down things one is grateful for, thereby shifting focus towards abundance and positivity. Meditation is another effective ritual that allows individuals to quiet the mind, connect with their inner wisdom, and visualize their desired outcomes with clarity and focus. By exploring these different types of manifestation rituals, individuals can choose the ones that resonate most with them and incorporate them into their daily practice.

When designing a manifestation ritual, it is essential to personalize it according to one's preferences, beliefs, and intentions. Begin by setting a clear intention or goal that you wish to manifest. This could be anything from attracting a fulfilling career to finding love or achieving inner peace. Once you have identified your intention, choose a manifestation ritual or combination of rituals that resonate with you.

Consider factors such as your preferred time of day, environment, and resources available when designing your ritual. For example, if you are a morning person, you may choose to incorporate your ritual into your morning routine, perhaps before starting your day. If you enjoy being outdoors, you might choose to perform your ritual in nature, surrounded by the beauty of the natural world. The key is to create a ritual that feels authentic and meaningful to you.

Consistency and commitment are integral aspects of any manifestation ritual. It is essential to commit to practicing your ritual regularly, ideally on a daily basis, to cultivate positive habits and reinforce your intentions. Consistency helps to maintain momentum and build energy towards your goals over time. Remember that manifestation is a journey, not a destination, and each ritual is a step forward on that journey.

To stay consistent, consider integrating your ritual into your daily routine and scheduling it at a specific time each day. This could be upon waking, before bed, or during a designated break. Additionally, hold yourself accountable by tracking your progress and celebrating your achievements along the way. By staying committed to your ritual, you will harness the power of consistency and unlock the full potential of manifestation in your life.

Manifestation rituals are potent tools for aligning with our desires, clarifying our intentions, and harnessing the power of the universe to co-create our reality. By exploring different types of rituals, designing a personalized practice, and committing to consistency, we can amplify the manifestation process and bring our dreams to fruition. Remember that manifestation is a journey of self-discovery and empowerment, and each ritual is an opportunity to connect with our highest potential and manifest our deepest desires.

The Power of Persistence

Embarking on the journey of manifestation is akin to setting sail on the vast sea of possibilities, where our desires and dreams await realization. However, navigating this journey requires not only clarity of intention but also unwavering consistency and persistence. In Chapter 8, we delve into the crucial role of maintaining consistency and persistence in the manifestation process, exploring strategies to overcome obstacles and cultivate resilience along the way.

Consistency serves as the cornerstone of manifestation, anchoring our intentions and actions in alignment with our desired outcomes. When we consistently focus our energy and attention on our goals, we create a powerful momentum that propels us forward towards their manifestation. Consistency fosters a sense of commitment and dedication, signaling to the universe our unwavering resolve to bring our dreams to fruition.

As we traverse the path of manifestation, we inevitably encounter challenges and obstacles that threaten to derail our progress. From self-doubt and fear to external distractions and setbacks, these hurdles can test our resolve and shake our confidence in the manifestation process. However, by recognizing these challenges as opportunities for growth and learning, we can navigate them with grace and resilience.

To maintain consistency and persistence on our manifestation journey, it is essential to employ practical strategies and techniques that keep us focused and motivated. Setting clear and achievable goals provides a roadmap for our journey, guiding our actions and decisions along the way. Effective time management ensures that we allocate our resources wisely, maximizing our productivity and progress. Additionally, accountability mechanisms, such as sharing our goals with a trusted friend or mentor, help keep us accountable and accountable, encouraging us to stay on track even when faced with challenges.

Resilience is the ability to bounce back from setbacks and challenges, emerging stronger and more determined than before. In the realm of manifestation, cultivating resilience is essential for overcoming obstacles and staying committed to our goals, even in the face of adversity. By embracing failure as a natural part of the journey and learning from our experiences, we develop the resilience needed to persevere in pursuit of our dreams. Cultivating self-compassion and practicing mindfulness can also help us navigate challenges with greater ease and grace, allowing us to maintain a positive outlook and unwavering faith in our ability to manifest our desires.

As we navigate the journey of manifestation, maintaining consistency and persistence is paramount to achieving our goals and realizing our dreams. By overcoming challenges with resilience and determination, we can stay focused on our intentions and continue to manifest our desired outcomes. With unwavering commitment and dedication, we harness the power of persistence to create a life filled with abundance, joy, and fulfillment.

Navigating Opportunities and Synchronicities on Your Manifestation Journey

In the intricate dance of manifestation, there exists a beautiful interplay between our intentions and the universe's response, often revealed through synchronicities and serendipitous opportunities. Chapter 8 delves into the profound concept of staying open to opportunities and synchronicities, exploring how these signs of alignment with the universe can propel us forward on our manifestation journey.

Flow is the state of effortless alignment with the universe, where our intentions seamlessly unfold and opportunities present themselves with ease. Synchronicity, coined by Carl Jung, refers to meaningful coincidences that defy logical explanation, serving as signs of alignment and guidance on our path. When we are in flow and attuned to synchronicities, we are in harmony with the rhythm of the universe, allowing manifestation to unfold organically.

Cultivating awareness is key to recognizing opportunities and synchronicities as they arise on our manifestation journey. Practices such as mindfulness meditation, journaling, and reflection can enhance our ability to tune into the subtle signals and signs that the universe presents. By quieting the mind and observing our thoughts and surroundings with curiosity and openness, we become more attuned to the flow of life and the synchronicities that guide us.

Trusting in the process of manifestation involves surrendering to the divine timing and unfolding of events, even when they deviate from our expectations or plans. It requires relinquishing control and embracing uncertainty, knowing that the universe has our best interests at heart. By releasing attachment to specific outcomes and remaining open to the infinite possibilities that exist, we invite greater flow and synchronicity into our lives.

While remaining open to opportunities and synchronicities is essential, taking inspired action is equally important in manifesting our desires. Inspired action involves acting from a place of alignment and intuition, guided by our inner wisdom and the signs provided by the universe. Whether it's pursuing a new opportunity, following a creative impulse, or taking a leap of faith, inspired action propels us closer to our manifestation goals and amplifies the flow of abundance in our lives.

Serendipitous events, often unexpected and seemingly random, are gifts from the universe that align with our intentions and desires. Embracing serendipity involves recognizing these moments of grace and seizing the opportunities they present, even if they initially appear unrelated to our goals. By remaining open and adaptable, we allow the magic of serendipity to unfold in our lives, leading us closer to our manifestation aspirations.

Staying open to opportunities and synchronicities is a fundamental aspect of the manifestation process, guiding us along the path towards our desires with grace and serendipity. By cultivating awareness, trusting the process, and taking inspired action, we align ourselves with the flow of the universe and invite greater abundance and fulfillment into our lives. As we embrace the magic of synchronicity and remain open to the infinite possibilities that exist, we unlock the door to unlimited potential and manifest our dreams with joy and ease.

The Transformative Power of Gratitude: Cultivating Abundance and Joy

In the tapestry of life, gratitude serves as a thread that weaves together moments of abundance, joy, and fulfillment. Chapter 9 delves into the profound practice of cultivating gratitude and appreciation, exploring its transformative power in manifesting abundance and deepening our connection with the universe.

Gratitude is a potent catalyst for transformation, capable of shifting our perspective from lack to abundance and illuminating the blessings that surround us. By acknowledging and appreciating the abundance already present in our lives, we open the floodgates to even greater blessings and manifestations.

The key to harnessing the power of gratitude lies in incorporating daily practices that cultivate a spirit of appreciation. Keeping a gratitude journal, where we record three things we are grateful for each day, serves as a powerful reminder of the abundance that exists in our lives. Additionally, practicing gratitude meditation allows us to quiet the mind and focus on the blessings that surround us, cultivating a sense of peace and contentment. Expressing appreciation to others through heartfelt gestures and words of thanks not only strengthens our relationships but also amplifies the positive energy we put out into the world.

At the heart of gratitude lies a profound shift in perspective—from scarcity to abundance. Rather than dwelling on what we lack, cultivating gratitude invites us to focus on what we have and cherish the blessings that grace our lives. By reframing our thoughts and perceptions, we create space for abundance to flow freely into our experience, manifesting a reality rich with blessings and opportunities.

Gratitude serves as a potent amplifier of the manifestation process, elevating our vibrational frequency and aligning us with the abundance of the universe. When we approach life with an attitude of gratitude, we attract positivity, prosperity, and joy into our experience. By fostering a deeper connection with the universe through acts of appreciation, we become co-creators of our reality, manifesting our desires with ease and grace.

Practical Tips for Cultivating Gratitude:

> Start and end each day with a gratitude practice, taking a moment to reflect on the blessings in your life.

> Keep a gratitude journal by your bedside and make it a habit to jot down things you are grateful for each morning or evening.

> Practice gratitude meditation regularly, focusing on feelings of appreciation and abundance as you breathe deeply and center yourself.

> Take time to express gratitude to others, whether through a heartfelt thank-you note, a kind gesture, or a simple word of appreciation.

> Practice mindfulness throughout the day, pausing to appreciate the beauty of nature, the warmth of the sun on your skin, or the laughter of loved ones.

Cultivating gratitude and appreciation is a transformative practice that has the power to enrich every aspect of our lives. By embracing gratitude as a way of being, we open ourselves to the abundance that surrounds us and invite greater blessings into our experience. As we harness the transformative power of gratitude, we elevate our vibration, amplify our manifestations, and co-create a reality filled with joy, abundance, and fulfillment.

Protecting Energy and Focusing Intentions

In the journey of manifestation, setting boundaries plays a crucial role in safeguarding our energy, maintaining focus, and honoring our personal needs and values. Chapter 10 explores the significance of boundaries in the manifestation process and provides practical guidance on setting and maintaining boundaries to align with our desires and goals.

Boundaries serve as protective barriers that shield us from energy drains, distractions, and influences that may hinder our manifestation efforts. By defining our limits and asserting our needs, we create space for focused intention and aligned action, allowing our manifestations to unfold with greater clarity and purpose.

Central to effective boundary-setting in manifestation is the process of setting clear intentions. Encouraging readers to clarify their desires, goals, and values, we empower them to establish boundaries that align with their highest aspirations. Whether it's setting boundaries around time, energy, or relationships, clear intentions serve as guiding lights that illuminate the path toward manifestation success.

One of the most challenging aspects of boundary-setting is learning to say no with love and compassion. Providing practical guidance, we explore strategies for asserting boundaries gracefully and respectfully, even in the face of external pressures or expectations. By honoring our own needs and priorities, we create space for the manifestation of our true desires and intentions.

Self-care lies at the heart of effective boundary-setting, serving as a cornerstone for maintaining healthy and sustainable manifestation practices. Emphasizing the importance of self-reflection, self-compassion, and assertive communication, we empower readers to prioritize their well-being while pursuing their manifestation goals. By nurturing themselves, individuals cultivate the inner strength and resilience needed to manifest their dreams with clarity and conviction.

Practical Tips for Setting Boundaries:

> Identify your values and priorities to establish boundaries that align with your highest aspirations.

> Communicate your boundaries clearly and assertively, using "I" statements to express your needs and preferences.

> Practice self-awareness and self-compassion to recognize when your boundaries are being tested or compromised.

> Set limits around your time, energy, and resources to protect against overcommitment and burnout.

> Surround yourself with supportive individuals who respect and honor your boundaries, and be prepared to distance yourself from those who do not.

Setting boundaries for manifestation is a powerful practice that empowers individuals to protect their energy, maintain focus, and honor their personal needs and values. By setting clear intentions, saying no with love, and prioritizing self-care, individuals create the necessary conditions for their manifestations to flourish. As we cultivate healthy boundaries, we pave the way for greater alignment, clarity, and fulfillment in our manifestation journey, allowing our deepest desires to manifest with ease and grace.

Chapter 9: Embracing Abundance Mindset

In a world often overshadowed by concerns of scarcity and limitation, there exists a profound shift in perspective—one that beckons us to embrace abundance in every aspect of our lives. In this chapter we embark on a transformative journey of self-discovery, empowerment, and boundless possibility.

At the heart of this chapter lies a fundamental truth: our mindset shapes our reality. When we choose to adopt an abundance mindset, we open ourselves to a wealth of opportunities, experiences, and blessings that await us. It is a mindset that celebrates abundance in all its forms—whether it be wealth, love, joy, or creativity—and invites us to recognize the infinite abundance that surrounds us each day.

As we delve into the pages of this chapter, we will explore the intricate interplay between abundance and scarcity mindsets, understanding how our beliefs and perceptions shape the world we inhabit. We will unravel the layers of conditioning and limitation that may have held us back, and in their place, cultivate a mindset of possibility, expansion, and unwavering faith in our inherent worthiness.

Through thought-provoking insights, practical exercises, and real-life examples, we will discover how to transcend fear and doubt, reclaiming our power to manifest the life of our dreams. From setting intentions and goals aligned with our deepest desires to cultivating resilience in the face of adversity, we will uncover the keys to unlocking our full potential and embracing abundance in every area of our lives.

But our journey does not end there. Beyond the realm of personal transformation lies a deeper truth: the profound impact of generosity and giving back. As we learn to celebrate our own abundance, we are called to share our blessings with others, creating a ripple effect of kindness, compassion, and goodwill that reverberates far and wide.

Nurturing an Abundance Mindset

In the tapestry of human consciousness, two contrasting paradigms shape our perceptions, beliefs, and ultimately, our reality: the abundance mindset and the scarcity mindset. These two lenses through which we view the world profoundly influence our behavior, decisions, and overall sense of well-being. In this article, we embark on a journey of exploration and discovery, seeking to understand the intricacies of these mindsets and their profound impact on our lives.

The Abundance Mindset

At its core, the abundance mindset is a perspective rooted in the belief that opportunities are limitless, resources are plentiful, and there is enough for everyone to thrive. Individuals who embody this mindset approach life with a sense of gratitude, recognizing the abundance that surrounds them in every moment. They view challenges as opportunities for growth, setbacks as temporary detours on the path to success, and success as something to be shared and celebrated with others.

Key characteristics of the abundance mindset include:

Gratitude: Those with an abundance mindset cultivate a deep sense of gratitude for the blessings in their lives, both big and small. They recognize the abundance of beauty, love, and opportunity that exists all around them, fostering a positive outlook on life.

Collaboration: Rather than viewing others as competitors, individuals with an abundance mindset see them as collaborators and allies on the journey to success. They believe in the power of cooperation and mutual support, understanding that by lifting others up, they elevate themselves in the process.

Optimism: An abundance mindset is characterized by optimism and a belief in the inherent goodness of life. Even in the face of challenges or setbacks, those with this mindset maintain a positive outlook, trusting in their ability to overcome obstacles and create the life they desire.

The Scarcity Mindset: Trapped in a Cycle of Fear and Limitation

In stark contrast to the abundance mindset, the scarcity mindset is rooted in the belief that resources are limited, opportunities are scarce, and one must compete fiercely to secure their share of the pie. Individuals operating from this mindset approach life with a sense of fear, anxiety, and a constant feeling of lack.

Key characteristics of the scarcity mindset include:

> Fear: Those with a scarcity mindset operate from a place of fear, constantly worrying about not having enough or losing what they already have. This fear-driven perspective leads to feelings of anxiety, stress, and a constant need to hoard resources for fear of scarcity.

> Competition: In a scarcity mindset, others are viewed as competitors rather than collaborators. There is a pervasive sense of competition and comparison, leading individuals to believe that someone else's success means less for them.

> Lack of Generosity: Individuals with a scarcity mindset struggle to share their resources or support others, fearing that doing so will diminish their own chances of success. This lack of generosity creates a sense of isolation and disconnect from the abundance that exists in the world.

The roots of our abundance or scarcity mindset can often be traced back to our early experiences, upbringing, and societal influences. From childhood, we absorb messages about the nature of success, worthiness, and abundance from our families, communities, and the media. These early conditioning experiences shape our beliefs and perceptions, laying the foundation for our mindset as adults.

For example, growing up in an environment where resources were scarce and competition was fierce may lead to the development of a scarcity mindset, characterized by a constant fear of not having enough or losing what one has. On the other hand, individuals raised in an environment that celebrates abundance, collaboration, and gratitude are more likely to adopt an abundance mindset, viewing the world as a place of infinite possibility and opportunity.

Cultivating an Abundance Mindset: Nurturing Seeds of Growth and Prosperity

While our early conditioning may influence our default mindset, it is essential to recognize that mindset is not fixed and can be shifted with intention and practice. By becoming aware of our thought patterns, beliefs, and behaviors, we can begin to challenge and reframe limiting beliefs that no longer serve us, replacing them with empowering beliefs that align with an abundance mindset.

Practical tips for cultivating an abundance mindset include:

Practice Gratitude: Take time each day to reflect on the blessings in your life and cultivate a sense of gratitude for the abundance that surrounds you.

Embrace Collaboration: Seek out opportunities to collaborate and support others on their journey to success, recognizing that their success does not diminish your own.

Focus on Solutions: Rather than dwelling on problems or limitations, shift your focus to solutions and possibilities, approaching challenges with a sense of curiosity and creativity.

Visualize Success: Use visualization techniques to imagine yourself achieving your goals and living a life of abundance, allowing yourself to feel the emotions associated with success.

Surround Yourself with Positivity: Surround yourself with people, experiences, and content that uplift and inspire you, feeding your mind with positivity and possibility.

Our mindset shapes our reality, and by embracing an abundance mindset, we open ourselves to a world of infinite possibility and opportunity. By understanding the key characteristics of both abundance and scarcity mindsets, we can begin to cultivate awareness and make conscious choices that align with our desired outcomes. With practice, patience, and a commitment to growth, we can nurture an abundance mindset that empowers us to manifest our dreams and create a life of fulfillment, joy, and prosperity.

Embracing the Power of Possibility: Cultivating an Abundance Mindset

In the tapestry of human consciousness, there exists a spectrum of mindsets that shape our perceptions, beliefs, and ultimately, our reality. At one end lies the scarcity mindset, steeped in fear, limitation, and a sense of lack. At the other end awaits the abundance mindset, a beacon of possibility, growth, and infinite potential. In this article, we embark on a journey of transformation, exploring practical strategies for cultivating a mindset of possibility and expansion that nurtures abundance in every aspect of our lives.

Shifting from Scarcity to Abundance: Strategies for Transformation

The journey from scarcity to abundance begins with a shift in perspective—a conscious choice to reframe negative thoughts, cultivate gratitude, and focus on possibilities rather than limitations. Here are some strategies to facilitate this transformation:

Reframing Negative Thoughts: The first step in cultivating an abundance mindset is to become aware of negative thought patterns and actively challenge them. Instead of dwelling on what we lack or fear, we can reframe our thoughts to focus on what is possible and within our control. For example, instead of thinking, "I'll never be successful," we can reframe it as, "I am capable of achieving my goals with dedication and effort."

Practicing Gratitude: Gratitude is a powerful antidote to scarcity mentality, shifting our focus from what we lack to what we have. By cultivating a daily gratitude practice—such as keeping a gratitude journal or expressing appreciation to others—we train our minds to recognize and appreciate the abundance that already exists in our lives.

Focusing on Possibilities: In every situation, there are endless possibilities waiting to be explored. By shifting our focus from limitations to possibilities, we open ourselves up to new opportunities and experiences. Instead of seeing challenges as roadblocks, we can view them as stepping stones on the path to growth and expansion.

Embracing a Growth Mindset: Learning, Development, and Resilience

Central to the abundance mindset is the concept of growth—a belief in our ability to learn, develop, and adapt to new circumstances. Here's how we can embrace a growth mindset in our daily lives:

Viewing Challenges as Opportunities: Instead of fearing failure or avoiding challenges, we can view them as opportunities for growth and learning. Every setback is a chance to build resilience, develop new skills, and emerge stronger than before. By reframing challenges as opportunities, we empower ourselves to overcome obstacles with confidence and determination.

Embracing Learning and Development: A growth mindset is rooted in a love of learning and a commitment to personal development. Instead of viewing our abilities as fixed, we see them as malleable and capable of improvement through effort and practice. By embracing lifelong learning and seeking out opportunities for growth, we unlock our full potential and create a path to success.

Cultivating Resilience: Resilience is the cornerstone of a growth mindset, enabling us to bounce back from setbacks and adapt to adversity. By cultivating resilience through self-care, positive coping strategies, and a support network, we build the inner strength needed to navigate life's challenges with grace and resilience.

Harnessing the Power of Visualization and Affirmations

Visualization and affirmations are powerful tools for reprogramming the subconscious mind and reinforcing an abundance mindset. Here's how to harness their power:

Visualizing Success: Visualization involves mentally rehearsing our desired outcomes and imagining them as already achieved. By vividly picturing our goals and desires, we create a clear mental image that aligns our thoughts, emotions, and actions with our intentions. Visualization activates the creative power of the subconscious mind, paving the way for manifestation and success.

> Using Affirmations: Affirmations are positive statements that we repeat to ourselves to reinforce empowering beliefs and overcome negative self-talk. By affirming our worthiness, abundance, and potential, we reprogram our subconscious mind with new beliefs that support our goals and aspirations. Affirmations serve as powerful reminders of our inherent value and potential, guiding us toward a mindset of abundance and possibility.

Cultivating an abundance mindset is a journey of self-discovery and transformation—a conscious choice to embrace possibility, growth, and infinite potential. By shifting our perspective, embracing a growth mindset, and harnessing the power of visualization and affirmations, we can unlock the door to abundance in every area of our lives. As we embrace the power of possibility, we step into a world of endless opportunities, where success, fulfillment, and abundance await.

Embracing Courage

In the labyrinth of life, fear and doubt often lurk in the shadows, casting a veil of uncertainty over our dreams and aspirations. They whisper tales of inadequacy, failure, and unworthiness, holding us back from realizing our true potential. Yet, beneath their guise lies the untapped reservoir of courage—the power to confront our fears, challenge our doubts, and step boldly into the unknown. In this article, we embark on a journey of self-discovery and empowerment, exploring practical strategies for letting go of fear and doubt as we navigate the path to success.

At the heart of fear and doubt lie deeply ingrained limiting beliefs— false narratives that shape our perceptions of ourselves and the world around us. To overcome these barriers, we must first shine a light on the shadows, uncovering the hidden beliefs that hold us back. Here are some exercises to help you identify and challenge limiting beliefs:

> Journaling Prompts: Set aside time to reflect on your thoughts and beliefs about success, worthiness, and abundance. Ask yourself probing questions such as:

> > What beliefs do I hold about my ability to succeed?

Do I believe I am worthy of achieving my goals and desires?

What fears or doubts arise when I think about pursuing my dreams?

Are there any past experiences or messages from others that have shaped my beliefs about success?

Belief Examination: Once you've identified your limiting beliefs, examine them with a critical eye. Challenge their validity by asking yourself:

Is this belief based on facts or assumptions?

What evidence do I have to support or refute this belief?

How has this belief impacted my actions and decisions in the past?

Is there an alternative belief that better serves my goals and aspirations?

Practicing Self-Compassion and Acceptance

As we confront our fears and doubts, it's essential to cultivate self-compassion—the gentle embrace of kindness, acceptance, and forgiveness toward ourselves. Here's how to practice self-compassion as you navigate your inner landscape:

Cultivate Self-Acceptance: Embrace all aspects of yourself, including your fears, insecurities, and imperfections. Recognize that you are inherently worthy and deserving of success, regardless of past mistakes or setbacks.

Practice Kindness and Forgiveness: Be gentle with yourself as you navigate your fears and insecurities. Treat yourself with the same kindness and compassion you would offer a dear friend facing similar challenges. Forgive yourself for past mistakes and failures, acknowledging that they are part of your growth journey.

Taking Courageous Action

Courage is not the absence of fear but the willingness to act in spite of it. As you confront your fears and doubts, remember that courage is not about being fearless—it's about feeling the fear and doing it anyway. Here's how to cultivate courage in the face of uncertainty:

> Take Small, Courageous Steps: Break your goals down into manageable tasks and take small, incremental steps toward your objectives. Each step, no matter how small, brings you closer to your dreams and builds momentum toward success.

> Embrace Uncertainty: Accept that uncertainty is a natural part of the journey toward success. Instead of letting fear of the unknown hold you back, embrace it as an opportunity for growth and exploration. Trust in your abilities and intuition to guide you forward, even when the path ahead is unclear.

> Lean Into Discomfort: Growth often lies on the other side of discomfort. Challenge yourself to step outside your comfort zone and embrace new experiences, even if they feel intimidating or unfamiliar. Remember that growth occurs when we stretch beyond our perceived limitations and embrace the unknown.

Letting go of fear and doubt is a courageous act of self-discovery and empowerment—a journey of reclaiming our inner strength, resilience, and confidence. By identifying and challenging limiting beliefs, practicing self-compassion and acceptance, and taking courageous action in the face of uncertainty, we can transcend our fears and doubts and step boldly into the light of our true potential. As we embrace courage as our compass, we unlock the door to limitless possibilities, where success, fulfillment, and abundance await.

The Power of Generosity

In a world often dominated by self-interest and competition, acts of generosity shine like beacons of light, illuminating the path to greater fulfillment, connection, and abundance. In this article, we delve into the transformative power of practicing generosity and giving back to others, exploring its myriad benefits for both the giver and the receiver, and offering practical suggestions for incorporating generosity into daily life.

Generosity is not merely an act of altruism; it is a profound expression of empathy, compassion, and interconnectedness. Research has shown that acts of kindness and generosity can have profound effects on our well-being, including:

Increased Happiness: Giving back triggers the release of endorphins, neurotransmitters that promote feelings of happiness and joy. When we extend kindness to others, we experience a natural "helper's high" that boosts our mood and overall sense of well-being.

Reduced Stress: Engaging in acts of generosity has been linked to lower levels of stress and anxiety. When we focus on helping others, we shift our attention away from our own worries and concerns, leading to greater emotional resilience and coping abilities.

Enhanced Sense of Connection: Giving back fosters a sense of connection and belonging, both to the recipients of our generosity and to the broader community. By reaching out and offering support to others, we strengthen our social bonds and forge deeper relationships based on trust and mutual respect.

Incorporating generosity into our daily lives doesn't require grand gestures or vast resources. Even the smallest acts of kindness can have a ripple effect, creating positive change in the world around us. Here are some practical suggestions for giving back:

Volunteer Your Time: Consider volunteering for a cause or organization that aligns with your values and interests. Whether it's serving meals at a homeless shelter, tutoring students, or participating in environmental clean-up efforts, volunteering offers a meaningful way to make a difference in your community.

Donate to Charity: Support organizations and initiatives that are working to create positive change in areas such as education, healthcare, environmental conservation, and social justice. Even small financial contributions can have a significant impact when pooled together with those of others.

Practice Random Acts of Kindness: Look for opportunities to brighten someone's day with random acts of kindness. This could be as simple as paying for the coffee of the person behind you in line, offering a compliment to a stranger, or helping an elderly neighbor with their groceries.

Share Your Skills and Talents: Identify ways to use your unique skills and talents to benefit others. Whether it's offering pro bono services to a nonprofit organization, sharing your expertise through mentoring or coaching, or teaching a workshop or class in your community, find ways to share your gifts with others.

Practicing generosity is not only an expression of abundance; it is also a powerful way to reinforce an abundance mindset—the belief that there is more than enough to go around for everyone. When we give freely without expectation of reciprocity, we affirm our belief in the abundance of resources, opportunities, and blessings available to us and others. By shifting our focus from scarcity to abundance, we open ourselves up to new possibilities and invite greater prosperity and fulfillment into our lives.

Practicing generosity and giving back to others is a profound act of self-discovery and empowerment—a journey of opening our hearts, expanding our perspectives, and embracing the interconnectedness of all beings. By extending kindness, compassion, and support to others, we not only enrich the lives of those around us but also experience greater joy, fulfillment, and abundance in our own lives. As we cultivate a spirit of generosity, we contribute to the creation of a more compassionate, equitable, and harmonious world—one act of kindness at a time.

Chapter 10: Surrendering to Divine Timing

In a world often characterized by hustle, ambition, and the pursuit of success, there exists a quieter, more profound truth: the universe has its own rhythm, its own timing, and its own plan for each of us. Welcome to Chapter 10 of our journey, where we delve into the profound wisdom of surrendering to divine timing.

Life has a way of unfolding in ways we cannot always predict or control. It's a journey filled with twists and turns, highs and lows, triumphs, and setbacks. Yet, amidst this unpredictability, there lies a deeper order—an unseen force that guides our path, orchestrating events with a wisdom far beyond our comprehension.

At the heart of surrendering to divine timing lies trust—in the universe, in God, or in a higher power, depending on one's beliefs. It's the profound recognition that there is a guiding force at work in our lives, leading us along our path with love and wisdom. Trust is the anchor that allows us to surrender control and relinquish the need to know every twist and turn that lies ahead. It's an act of faith—a leap into the unknown, guided by the belief that all is unfolding exactly as it should.

Yet, trust is often tested by our attachment to specific outcomes. We set goals, make plans, and envision our ideal futures with unwavering clarity. But what happens when life takes an unexpected turn? When our carefully laid plans unravel, and the outcomes we desire seem out of reach? It is here that we are called to release our attachment—to let go of our grip on the future and surrender to the present moment. It's an invitation to loosen our grasp on what we think should be and embrace what is, knowing that in doing so, we open ourselves up to infinite possibilities.

Patience is a virtue often tested on the path of surrender. In a world that values instant gratification and quick results, the concept of waiting can feel like anathema. Yet, patience is the key to surrendering to divine timing. It's the willingness to trust in the unfolding of events, even when they seem to move at a glacial pace. Patience invites us to embrace the journey—the highs and lows, the twists and turns—as essential elements of our growth and evolution.

It's a gentle reminder that everything happens in its own time, according to a plan far grander than our own.

In the tapestry of life, there are moments of serendipity—unexpected, fortuitous events that seem to occur by chance. These moments are not accidents but rather divine interventions—subtle nudges from the universe guiding us along our path. Whether it's a chance encounter, a timely opportunity, or a stroke of luck, serendipity reminds us that we are not alone—that the universe is conspiring in our favor, even when we least expect it. All we need to do is remain open, receptive, and attuned to the signs and signals that surround us.

Surrendering to divine timing is not about passive resignation or giving up on our dreams. It's about embracing the flow of life—trusting that everything is happening for our highest good, even when we cannot see the bigger picture. It's about finding peace in the midst of uncertainty, joy in the face of adversity, and gratitude for the blessings that abound, even in the darkest of times.

Life is akin to a river, flowing with its own rhythm and currents. Just as a river meanders through valleys and plains, encountering obstacles and bends along the way, so too does our journey through life. And just as a river eventually finds its way to the sea, so too do we find our way to our truest selves, guided by the gentle current of divine timing.

Divine timing is not bound by clocks or calendars. It operates on a higher plane—a plane where past, present, and future merge into one timeless moment. It is the moment when synchronicities align, opportunities arise, and miracles unfold. It is the moment when we recognize that everything is happening exactly as it should—that every setback, every detour, every delay is a stepping stone on the path to our highest good.

At the heart of surrendering to divine timing lies the gift of presence—the gift of being fully immersed in the here and now. In the present moment, there is no past to regret, no future to worry about—only the infinite expanse of possibility stretching out before us. It is here, in this eternal now, that we find peace, joy, and contentment.

As you journey through the waters of surrender, remember to honor your inner wisdom—the quiet voice that whispers guidance in the depths of your soul. Trust in the wisdom of your intuition, the wisdom of your heart, and the wisdom of your spirit. For it is through this inner guidance that you will navigate the currents of life with grace and ease.

In the dance of surrender, we relinquish our need for control and embrace the wisdom of the universe. We trust in the unseen forces that guide our path, release attachment to outcomes, and surrender to the flow of life. And in doing so, we discover the profound truth that in surrendering to divine timing, we are guided, supported, and infinitely loved every step of the way.

Embracing Faith in the Universe

In the tapestry of life, there exists an unseen hand that weaves the threads of our existence with purpose and precision. Whether we call it the universe, God, Source, or a higher power, there is a force beyond our comprehension guiding our journey with infinite wisdom and love. Trusting in this divine presence requires a leap of faith—a surrendering of control and a deepening of faith in the inherent goodness of life.

At times, life may seem like a labyrinth of confusion and chaos, leaving us questioning the purpose behind our struggles and setbacks. Yet, in the depths of uncertainty, there lies a profound truth: there is a greater plan at work, far beyond our limited perception. Just as a painter meticulously crafts a masterpiece stroke by stroke, so too does the universe orchestrate the intricate details of our lives with divine precision. Trusting in this greater plan means surrendering to the flow of life, knowing that every twist and turn serves a purpose in the grand design of our journey.

In our modern world filled with hustle and bustle, it's easy to fall into the trap of believing that success and fulfillment are solely dependent on our efforts and actions. Yet, the truth is, there is only so much we can control. The rest is left to the hands of fate, the unfolding of divine timing, and the guidance of the universe. Learning to relinquish control and surrender to the wisdom of the cosmos is a profound act of faith—one that allows us to release the burden of responsibility and embrace the freedom of trust. When we surrender our need to micromanage every aspect of our lives, we open ourselves up to the infinite possibilities that await us.

Throughout our lives, we may encounter moments of profound trust and faith in the universe—moments that affirm our belief in the inherent goodness of life and the divine orchestration of our journey. These moments may come in the form of synchronicities, serendipitous encounters, or unexpected blessings that remind us of the magic that surrounds us. For some, it may be the timely arrival of a long-awaited opportunity, while for others, it may be the gentle nudge of intuition guiding them down the path less traveled. Whatever form they may take, these moments serve as beacons of light, illuminating our path and reaffirming our trust in the universe's benevolent guidance.

Trusting in the universe, God, or a higher power requires a willingness to embrace the unknown—to venture into uncharted territory with courage and conviction. It means surrendering to the divine flow of life, even when the waters are murky and the path ahead is uncertain. In the face of adversity, it means holding steadfast to the belief that everything is happening for our highest good, even when we cannot see the bigger picture. And in moments of doubt and despair, it means turning inward and reconnecting with the spark of divinity that resides within us, knowing that we are never alone on this journey.

In life, trust serves as the melody that guides our steps and soothes our souls. It is the anchor that keeps us grounded amidst life's storms and the beacon that lights our way through the darkness. As we navigate the twists and turns of our journey, may we remember to trust in the wisdom of the universe, knowing that we are held in the loving embrace of a force far greater than ourselves. And in this trust, may we find peace, purpose, and profound joy in the unfolding of our divine destiny.

Liberating Yourself from Attachment to Outcomes

In the pursuit of our goals and desires, it's natural to envision specific outcomes and strive for their realization with unwavering determination. However, there exists a delicate balance between setting intentions and becoming overly attached to the results. When we cling too tightly to our desired outcomes, we inadvertently create resistance and block the natural flow of manifestation. In this article, we will explore the detrimental effects of attachment to outcomes, examine the paradox of manifestation, and offer practical strategies for releasing attachment and embracing the flow of life.

Attachment to specific outcomes can have detrimental effects on our well-being and the manifestation process. When we become fixated on a particular outcome, we may experience heightened stress, anxiety, and fear of failure. Our happiness and sense of self-worth become contingent upon the achievement of our goals, leading to a constant state of striving and dissatisfaction. Moreover, attachment narrows our focus and blinds us to alternative paths and opportunities that may lead to even greater fulfillment and success.

While setting intentions and goals is an essential aspect of manifestation, clinging too tightly to specific outcomes can hinder our progress. This paradox lies at the heart of the manifestation process: the more we strive to control and manipulate outcomes, the more we resist the natural flow of manifestation. It is only when we surrender our attachment and trust in the inherent wisdom of the universe that we allow space for miracles to unfold and blessings to manifest in unexpected ways.

Practical Strategies for Releasing Attachment

Releasing attachment to outcomes requires a conscious effort to let go of expectations and surrender to the present moment. Here are some practical strategies to help you cultivate a mindset of detachment and embrace the flow of life:

> **Practice Mindfulness:** Cultivate present-moment awareness through mindfulness practices such as meditation, deep breathing, and body scans. By anchoring yourself in the present moment, you can release attachment to the past and future and find peace in the here and now.

> **Let Go of Expectations:** Release the need for specific outcomes by embracing uncertainty and welcoming whatever unfolds with an open heart and mind. Trust that the universe has a plan far beyond your limited perception, and surrender to the divine timing of manifestation.

> **Surrender to the Process:** Instead of focusing solely on the destination, embrace the journey with all its twists and turns. Trust that every experience, whether perceived as positive

or negative, is a stepping stone on the path to your highest good.

Practice Gratitude: Cultivate an attitude of gratitude for the blessings and opportunities that come your way, regardless of whether they align with your preconceived expectations. By focusing on what you already have, you shift your energy from lack to abundance and attract more blessings into your life.

As you release attachment to outcomes and surrender to the flow of life, you will experience a sense of liberation and freedom unlike anything you've ever known. Instead of fighting against the currents of existence, you will learn to navigate the ebbs and flows with grace and ease. In this state of surrender, you will discover a profound sense of peace, contentment, and inner fulfillment that transcends the attainment of any external goal.

In the dance of manifestation, detachment is the key that unlocks the door to true freedom and fulfillment. By releasing attachment to specific outcomes and embracing the flow of life, you open yourself up to infinite possibilities and allow the universe to work its magic in mysterious ways. So, let go of your expectations, surrender to the process, and trust in the divine timing of manifestation. In doing so, you will find liberation, joy, and abundance beyond your wildest dreams.

Cultivating Patience and Trust in the Process

In a world that moves at a relentless pace, patience has become a rare and precious virtue. Yet, it is precisely in our moments of waiting, of surrendering to the ebb and flow of life, that we often find our greatest lessons and blessings. In this article, we will explore the art of embracing patience and trust in the process, surrendering to divine timing, and discovering the profound wisdom that comes from allowing things to unfold in their own time.

Patience is more than just the ability to wait; it is a state of inner calm and acceptance that allows us to gracefully navigate life's uncertainties and challenges. In a world that demands instant gratification and immediate results, patience reminds us to slow down, breathe, and trust in the unfolding of divine timing. It is the antidote to anxiety, frustration, and impatience, offering us the serenity to embrace each moment with grace and gratitude.

Divine timing is the belief that everything happens in its own time, according to a higher plan or purpose that is beyond our understanding. It is the recognition that there is a greater intelligence at work in the universe, orchestrating the events of our lives in perfect harmony. When we surrender to divine timing, we let go of our need to control and manipulate outcomes, trusting that everything is unfolding exactly as it should, for our highest good.

Cultivating Patience

Cultivating patience is a practice that requires mindfulness, self-awareness, and a willingness to surrender to the present moment. Here are some tips for cultivating patience in your life:

Practice Mindfulness: Cultivate present-moment awareness through mindfulness practices such as meditation, deep breathing, and body scans. By anchoring yourself in the present moment, you can let go of worries about the future and regrets about the past, finding peace and contentment in the here and now.

Reframe Challenges as Opportunities: Instead of viewing challenges as obstacles to be overcome, reframe them as opportunities for growth and learning. Embrace setbacks and difficulties as valuable lessons that can strengthen your resilience and deepen your wisdom.

Stay Present: Resist the temptation to constantly project into the future or dwell on the past. Instead, stay present in each moment, fully engaged with whatever is unfolding before you. By staying present, you can cultivate gratitude for the blessings that surround you and find joy in the simple pleasures of life.

Trusting in the Process

Trusting in the process means relinquishing our need for certainty and control, and embracing the inherent wisdom of the universe. It is the recognition that even in the midst of uncertainty and doubt, there is a divine order at work, guiding us toward our highest destiny. When we trust in the process, we surrender our fears and insecurities, allowing ourselves to be carried forward by the currents of grace and love.

Throughout history, spiritual traditions have emphasized the importance of patience and trust in the process. From the Taoist concept of Wu Wei, or effortless action, to the Christian notion of "Thy will be done," wisdom traditions teach us to surrender to the flow of life and trust in the inherent goodness of the universe. When we align ourselves with these timeless teachings, we find peace, purpose, and meaning in the midst of life's uncertainties.

In a world that moves at breakneck speed, patience and trust in the process have become rare and precious commodities. Yet, it is precisely in our moments of waiting, of surrendering to divine timing, that we often find our greatest wisdom and growth. So, as you navigate the ups and downs of life, remember to embrace patience, trust in the process, and surrender to the unfolding of divine timing. In doing so, you will discover a profound sense of peace, purpose, and fulfillment beyond measure.

Embracing Serendipity and Divine Intervention: Navigating Life's Fortuitous Encounters

In the grand tapestry of life, there are moments when unexpected events unfold, seemingly by chance, yet carrying profound significance and meaning. These moments, known as serendipity, and the belief in divine intervention remind us that there is a higher order at work in the universe, guiding our path and orchestrating synchronicities that lead us toward our destiny. In this article, we will explore the concept of serendipity and divine intervention, share stories of remarkable encounters, and discuss the importance of remaining open to the magic of life's unexpected twists and turns.

Serendipity is often described as the occurrence of fortunate events by chance, leading to unexpected discoveries or opportunities. It is the delightful surprise of stumbling upon something wonderful when least expected, whether it's meeting a kindred spirit, finding a solution to a problem, or experiencing a moment of profound insight. Divine intervention, on the other hand, refers to the belief that these serendipitous events are not mere coincidences but are instead guided by a higher power or intelligence. It is the recognition that there is a divine plan at work in our lives, unfolding in ways that are beyond our comprehension.

Serendipitous moments often occur when we least expect them, catching us off guard and leaving us in awe of life's mysterious ways. These moments can take many forms, from chance encounters with strangers who become lifelong friends, to stumbling upon opportunities that align perfectly with our dreams and aspirations. One such story is that of Sarah, who, while lost in a new city, stumbled upon a quaint bookstore where she found a book that changed the course of her life. Serendipity reminds us to remain open, curious, and receptive to the unexpected gifts that life has to offer.

Divine intervention goes beyond the realm of chance encounters, suggesting that there is a guiding force at work in the universe, directing our steps and leading us toward our highest good. It is the belief that everything happens for a reason, and that even the most challenging circumstances can ultimately lead to blessings in disguise. Take the story of Michael, who narrowly missed a flight, only to discover later that the plane had encountered mechanical issues mid-flight. Divine intervention reminds us to trust in the inherent wisdom of the universe and to surrender to the flow of life's unfolding.

The key to experiencing serendipity and divine intervention lies in remaining open, receptive, and attuned to the subtle signs and signals from the universe. This means letting go of rigid expectations and allowing ourselves to be guided by intuition and inner wisdom. It means trusting that even in the midst of uncertainty, there is a higher purpose at work, leading us toward our destiny. By remaining open to the magic of life's unexpected twists and turns, we invite serendipity and divine intervention to grace our lives with their presence.

In a world that often feels chaotic and uncertain, serendipity and divine intervention remind us that there is a greater intelligence at work in the universe, guiding our path and weaving the threads of our lives into a beautiful tapestry of experiences. Whether it's a chance encounter with a stranger, a stroke of luck, or a moment of profound insight, these moments of synchronicity remind us that we are not alone, and that there is a deeper meaning and purpose to our existence. So, as you journey through life, remember to remain open, receptive, and attuned to the magic of serendipity and divine intervention. Who knows what wonders await just around the corner?

Manifesting Your Destiny: Reflect, Embrace, and Thrive

Embarking on a journey of manifestation is not merely about achieving tangible outcomes; it's about the transformation that occurs within us along the way. As we reach the conclusion of this transformative journey, it's essential to pause and reflect on the path we've traveled, the lessons we've learned, and the abundance we've discovered within ourselves and the world around us.

Reflecting on our manifestation journey allows us to appreciate the progress we've made and the hurdles we've overcome. It's an opportunity to acknowledge the inner strength, resilience, and determination that have propelled us forward. Take a moment to revisit the goals you set, the intentions you planted, and the actions you took to manifest your desires. Celebrate the milestones you've achieved, no matter how small, and recognize the growth that has unfolded within you.

Self-reflection is a powerful tool for gaining insight into our experiences. Take time to ponder the lessons learned throughout your manifestation journey. What challenges did you encounter, and how did you navigate them? What limiting beliefs did you uncover, and how did you overcome them? Reflecting on these questions allows us to glean wisdom from our experiences and carry it forward on our journey toward greater abundance and fulfillment.

Expressing gratitude for the manifestations that have already come into fruition cultivates a mindset of abundance and appreciation. Take inventory of the blessings in your life, both big and small, and express gratitude for each one. Gratitude not only attracts more abundance into our lives but also deepens our sense of contentment and fulfillment.

Journaling about your manifestation journey is a powerful way to capture your experiences and insights. Use your journal as a space to record your thoughts, feelings, and observations along the way. Document the synchronicities, signs, and moments of clarity that have guided you on your path. Reflecting on your journal entries allows you to track your growth over time and gain perspective on your journey.

As we reflect on our manifestation journey, we recognize that abundance extends far beyond material wealth. True abundance encompasses all aspects of our lives—our relationships, health, well-being, and sense of purpose. Embracing abundance means recognizing the abundance that already exists within us and around us and aligning with the flow of universal abundance.

Take inventory of the abundance in your life, from the love and support of friends and family to the beauty of nature that surrounds you. Recognize that abundance comes in many forms and is not limited to financial wealth. Cultivate an abundance mindset by focusing on what you have rather than what you lack, and by embracing a sense of gratitude for the blessings in your life.

As we conclude our manifestation journey, it's important to remember that manifestation is not a one-time event but an ongoing practice. Continue to set intentions, visualize your goals, and take inspired action toward your desires. Trust in the process, stay open to possibilities, and remain aligned with your highest vision for yourself and your life.

Reflecting on our manifestation journey allows us to honor the progress we've made, the lessons we've learned, and the abundance we've discovered along the way. As we embrace abundance in all areas of our lives and continue the practice of manifestation, we step into a future filled with limitless potential and infinite possibilities.

Cultivating Wealth in Every Aspect of Life

When we think of abundance, our minds often gravitate toward material wealth—money, possessions, and tangible assets. However, true abundance extends far beyond the realm of material possessions. It encompasses the richness of our relationships, the vitality of our health, the depth of our joy, and the fulfillment of our purpose. In this article, we explore the importance of embracing abundance in all areas of life and offer practical tips for cultivating an abundance mindset.

Abundance is not limited to financial prosperity; it encompasses every facet of our existence. It is the abundance of love in our relationships, the abundance of vitality in our health, the abundance of joy in our experiences, and the abundance of meaning in our lives. By expanding our definition of abundance, we open ourselves up to the myriad blessings that surround us each day.

Take a moment to pause and reflect on the abundance that already exists in your life. Consider the love and support of friends and family, the beauty of nature that surrounds you, and the opportunities for growth and learning that present themselves each day. By acknowledging and appreciating the abundance that surrounds us, we shift our focus from scarcity to abundance and cultivate a mindset of gratitude and abundance.

Practical Tips for Cultivating Abundance Mindset:

Practice Gratitude: Cultivate a daily gratitude practice by acknowledging and appreciating the blessings in your life, both big and small. Keep a gratitude journal or take a few moments each day to reflect on what you are grateful for. Gratitude is the gateway to abundance, as it shifts our focus from what we lack to what we have.

Foster Meaningful Connections: Invest time and energy into building and nurturing meaningful relationships with others. Surround yourself with people who uplift and inspire you, and cultivate deep connections based on trust, respect, and authenticity. The richness of our relationships is a true measure of abundance in our lives.

Prioritize Self-Care and Well-Being: Take care of your physical, mental, and emotional well-being by prioritizing self-care practices. Make time for activities that nourish your body, mind, and soul, whether it's exercise, meditation, creative expression, or simply spending time in nature. When we prioritize our well-being, we create a foundation of abundance from which all other aspects of our lives can flourish.

Focus on What You Can Control: Instead of dwelling on what you lack or what is beyond your control, focus your energy on what you can influence and change. Set goals and take proactive steps toward achieving them, knowing that abundance is within your reach when you align your actions with your intentions.

Train your mind to focus on the positive aspects of life and adopt a mindset of abundance and possibility. Challenge negative thoughts and beliefs that may be holding you back, and replace them with affirmations and empowering beliefs that support your vision for abundance.

Embracing abundance in all areas of life is a mindset and a way of being that allows us to fully experience the richness and beauty of our existence. By expanding our definition of abundance, recognizing the blessings that surround us, and cultivating an abundance mindset, we open ourselves up to a life filled with joy, fulfillment, and infinite possibilities.

The Everlasting Journey of Manifestation: Continuity in Creation

Manifestation is not merely a fleeting moment of wishful thinking; it is an ongoing journey of conscious creation that requires dedication, perseverance, and a steadfast belief in the power of intention. In this article, we delve into the importance of continuing the practice of manifestation, offering guidance on refining and evolving your approach to manifesting your desires.

Manifestation is not a one-time event but a lifelong practice of aligning your thoughts, beliefs, and actions with your deepest desires and intentions. It is a journey of self-discovery and personal growth, where each manifestation serves as a stepping stone toward greater fulfillment and expansion. By embracing manifestation as a continuous practice, you acknowledge that your journey is ever-evolving and that there is always room for growth and refinement.

As you continue on your manifestation journey, take time to reflect on your goals, intentions, and desires. Are there new aspirations that have emerged? Are there areas of your life that you would like to focus on more deeply? Refine your manifestation practice by setting new goals, intentions, and desires that resonate with your evolving vision for your life. Allow yourself to dream big and to envision a future that is aligned with your highest aspirations.

One of the keys to successful manifestation is to remain open and receptive to new possibilities and opportunities that may arise along the way. Trust in the process of manifestation and the wisdom of the universe, knowing that the universe has a way of orchestrating events and synchronicities in alignment with your intentions. Stay open-minded and curious, and be willing to explore new avenues and pathways that may lead you closer to your goals.

To continue the practice of manifestation, it is essential to integrate manifestation techniques into your daily life. Incorporate practices such as visualization, affirmations, and gratitude into your daily routine to reinforce your intentions and align your energy with your desires. Visualize yourself living the life of your dreams, affirm your worthiness and abundance, and express gratitude for the blessings that are already present in your life. By integrating manifestation techniques into your daily life, you infuse every moment with the energy of creation and possibility.

As you embark on the journey of manifestation, remember that it is not a destination but a continuous process of growth, expansion, and self-discovery. By refining and evolving your manifestation practice, remaining open to new possibilities, and integrating manifestation techniques into your daily life, you can continue to manifest your desires and create the life you truly desire. Embrace the journey with an open heart and a spirit of curiosity, knowing that the universe is always conspiring in your favor.

About the Author

Aria Rivers, a debut author offers practical wisdom and transformative insights for those seeking fulfillment and prosperity. With a compassionate voice and relatable approach, Aria guides readers on a journey of self-discovery and empowerment, sharing tools and exercises to unlock their fullest potential. With a deep passion for personal growth and spiritual exploration, Aria brings a fresh perspective to the realm of manifestation, blending ancient wisdom with modern insights to empower readers to unlock their fullest potential.

Drawing from her own experiences and profound understanding of universal principles, Aria offers practical guidance, inspiring anecdotes, and powerful exercises that guide readers step-by-step on their manifestation journey.

www.ingramcontent.com/pod-product-compliance
Lightning Source LLC
LaVergne TN
LVHW091720190726
843493LV00001B/375